Conqueror

CONQUEROR

Rob Griffin

The Crowood Press

First published in 1999 by
The Crowood Press Ltd
Ramsbury, Marlborough
Wiltshire SN8 2HR

British Library Cataloguing-in-Publication Data
A catalogue record for this book is available from the British Library.

ISBN 1 86126 251 5

Photograph previous page: 'Eaglet' pauses for a photo call. The vehicle is short of
front mudguards, rear outer bazooka plate and all inner bazooka plates.

Typeset by Textype Typesetters, Cambridge

Printed and bound by T.J. International, Padstow

Contents

1 Conqueror Development

THE CONQUEROR'S PREDECESSORS

The path that the modern tank designer must travel is almost as tortuous and stony as the ground that his vehicle will one day travel over, and perhaps no modern vehicle illustrates this better than the Conqueror heavy gun tank.

Great Britain invented the tank during the First World War, and for a period was the leading exponent of tank design and tactics. However, once the war was over many different influences were brought to bear which seemed to sound the death knell for the fledgling Tank Corps and its new weapon. Predictably, some of the opposition came from the old school of the mounted cavalry, who, whilst praising what the tank had achieved, pointed out that it was only a short-term weapon developed because of trench warfare. Such a type of warfare would never happen again, they claimed, thus the horse could return to the battlefield again. Although these comments were voiced loud and often, wiser heads realized that the horse was finished as a means of conducting war on a modern battlefield.

Of more concern was the big enemy of the Treasury, which was rightly concerned with trying to balance Britain's post-war budget and help the country back to a peacetime environment. As always, the first casualty was defence, resulting in 1922 in the regiments disbanding and being amalgamated. The Royal Tank Corps with its expensive machinery that was now redundant because we had just won the 'war to end all wars'

The beginning. A WWI tank, in this instance a Female denoted by the machine guns that can be seen in the sponson. Note the rhomboidal shape with the track going completely around the body, also the wooden roof-shaped frame on top of the vehicle. This would have had netting attached to it to try to prevent the enemy throwing explosive devices onto the roof of the tank. Tank Museum.

seemed to be a suitable case for cost-cutting. Fortunately, the Corps had some powerful friends and after much lobbying it survived, but the cost-cutting still took place, falling on the development of vehicles, a decision that was to have a fearful effect on British tank crews in twenty years' time.

Due to the political restraints applied by very blinkered politicians, the new tanks that were created were of such inferior quality that the nation that had invented the tank slipped further behind the world with every new vehicle produced. It was the policy of using little two-men 'tankettes' armed at best with a machine gun that left the British Army with vehicles that were little more than death traps once war became inevitable once again.

Meanwhile, the defeated Germans, although banned from making and using tanks, had learned from their experiences and had set about creating what would become famous as their *Panzer* armies. When war came to Europe once more and the Allied armies came face to face with the Germans, luck was on Germany's side. Not for the first time, the Allies had overestimated the strength of the enemy, and the lack of a central Allied command worked in the Germans' favour. Had the Allies placed less emphasis on national command, the Germans may well have been stopped in France in 1940. Britain was fielding numerous light tanks such as the Mk VI with two machine guns which were ideal for recce but not for tank-to-tank combat. Also deployed were two marks of the Infantry tank Matilda, the Mk I and Mk II. The less said about the Mk I the better, but the

A Carden Lloyd tankette. This is the type of vehicle that the War Office became increasingly interested in during the inter-war years, not for any great advances in armour technology but for the fact that it was cheap. No thought about sending men to fight an enemy that would probably be far better equipped and armed seemed to have been entertained. Tank Museum.

Light Tank MkVI

Length	11ft 9in
Width	6ft 9in
Height	7ft 4in
Weight	11,650lb
Power	Meadows 6-cylinder petrol 88bhp
Crew	3
Armament	1 x .5in Vickers machine gun
Secondary armament	1 x .303 Vickers machine gun
Armour	Max 0.55in Min 0.23in
Speed	34mph

Notes The British entered the war with several versions of this light tank that had started life in 1930. Although it was very fast it was lightly armoured and armed. Service in France soon showed up its weakness and in 1940 the light tank was deleted from British Armoured divisions. It did, however, serve on in the desert as a reconnaissance vehicle.

A little better and starting to look like a tank but still woefully inadequate. This is the Vickers Mk VI light tank that was sent to France to try to stop the Germans. At its best, it was armed with a 15mm machine gun against the German's 20mm cannon and 50mm tank guns. Tank Museum.

The Matilda Mk 1. When General Elles first saw this he is reputed to have said, 'it waddles like Matilda' (Matilda was a duck cartoon character of the time) so the name stuck. It was crewed by two men armed with a machine gun, and though for its time it had very good armour, it was hopelessly outclassed in France. Tank Museum.

The Matilda II. Quite rightly this was called the Queen of the Battlefield during the early years of the War. It proved a nasty surprise to the Germans when they found that their armour piercing rounds were bouncing off its thick armour, and it was only the emergency deployment of the 88mm anti aircraft gun in a ground role that finally managed to pierce the armour. Tank Museum

Matilda Mk I

Length	15ft 11in
Width	7ft 6in
Height	6ft 2in
Weight	24,605lb
Power	Ford V8 petrol 70bhp
Crew	2
Armament	1 x .303 Vickers machine gun, later 1 x .50 Vickers
Secondary armament	none
Armour	Max 2.36in min 0.39in
Speed	8mph

Notes Introduced in 1936 at a design price not to exceed £6,000. the Armoured Corps was left with a heavily armoured vehicle for the period that mounted only a machine gun. It went to war in France where it soon was proved to be hopelessly outclassed. Those that survived were relegated to training vehicles.

Mk II, which later gained fame in the Western Desert, at last restored some measure of pride in the British tank design teams. Armed with a Besa machine gun and a two-pounder gun with maximum armour of 3in (75mm) it was impervious to any anti-tank gun used by the Germans. At the Battle of Arras the 4th and 7th Royal Tank Regiment inflicted a very nasty shock on the German *Panzers* which found that their armour-piercing rounds were just bouncing off the Matilda's thick armour. Only the last minute deployment of the 88mm (3.5in) anti-aircraft gun, which penetrated the Matilda's armour easily, saved the day for the Germans. This action, however, had given the Germans a severe shock and after examining examples of the Matilda they decided that large guns and armour protection had to be the way forwards. The British also took in this point but not as rapidly, and it would take events in North Africa to speed things up.

To trace Conqueror's development we must go as

Matilda Mk II

Length	18ft 5in
Width	8ft 6in
Height	8ft 3in
Weight	59360lb
Power	2 x AEC 6 cylinder diesel 190bhp
Crew	4
Armament	2-pounder
Secondary armament	1 x 7.92 Besa machine gun
Armour	Max 3.07in min 0.55in
Speed	15.5mph

Notes The Matilda II was a vast improvement on the Mk I, although it still gave the British a tank that was heavily armoured but lightly armed. Its size was still governed by the rail width restrictions. However, this is the tank that scared Rommel and the Germans at the battle of Arras. It was also the only British tank that saw continuous service throughout the war in one form or another.

This was an attempt to up-gun the successful Churchill so that it could take the lethal 17-pounder. The Black Prince was based on Churchill-proven technology so would probably have run all right, but it was not the vehicle that was needed at the time and events overtook it. Only six were built.

far back as 1943. It had at last been realized that British tank design up till then had been, at the best, mediocre, and it said a lot for the tank crews that they had actually scored some successes with them, but always at a considerable loss in valuable tank crews. One has only to read any of the excellent books written by 'men who were there' to realize the heroism displayed. The inescapable equation, however, was that while vehicles could be replaced, eventually the army would run out of crews.

The pressing need for the Allies was to produce a vehicle that could be fitted with a high-velocity gun that would enable them to defeat current German armour along with anything that was projected to come into service in the foreseeable future. It was also to provide the crews with a high level of protection. At this juncture, the lack of government funding for tank development prior to the war meant that no vehicle in the British inventory was suitable for the required up-gunning. One other problem that effectively prevented the British from up-gunning was the restrictions placed on the width of the vehicle. This was enforced to allow vehicles being carried by rail to fit the width gauge as prescribed by the railway.

As an interim measure underlying the need to get a big gun into service as soon as possible a Churchill tank was converted to carry a 3in (76mm) gun fitted to a large box superstructure instead of a conventional turret. However, this really only produced a self-propelled gun which would have been at an immense disadvantage in a tank-to-tank battle.

The Black Prince

This left only one solution – a brand new vehicle had to be produced. The end result of this was the A43 project which produced the Black Prince. To all intents and purposes, this was nothing more than a scaled-up Churchill, which, thanks at last to the removal of the width restriction, meant that it could be armed with a formidable gun, the deadly 17-pounder. Such a weapon should have been the answer to tank crews' prayers. However, in the words of one old gunnery instructor who was a member of the trials team, 'Black Prince could not hit the side of a barn door even if the barn door was right in front of the tank.' To be fair to the tank, it would seem that so much time had been lavished on getting the right gun that not a lot of thought had been given to producing a decent fire-control system to support it.

Other problems that arose were the fact that the vehicle came under severe criticism, not least from the DRAC (Director of the Royal Armoured Corps) for the decision to fit the Bedford engine from

---

Churchill III

Length	25ft 2in
Width	10ft 8in
Height	8ft 2in
Weight	39 tons
Power	Bedford 12-cylinder petrol 350bhp
Crew	5
Armament	75mm
Secondary armament	2x 7.92 Besa machine guns
Armour	Max 4in min 0.62in
Speed	16mph

Notes Churchill was designed around the principle of the Infantry tank, and was heavily armoured to be able to support the Infantry in the close support role. It was, however, poorly armed, starting life with just the 2-

	Black Prince
Length	28ft 11in
Width	11ft 4in
Height	9ft
Weight	112,000lb
Power	Bedford horizontally opposed 12-cylinder petrol 35bhp
Crew	5
Armament	17-pounder
Secondary armament	2x 7.92 Besa machine guns
Armour	Max 3.46in Min 0.70in
Speed	12mph

Notes Black Prince was an attempt to up-gun the Churchill with the 17-pounder, but it was really just a scaled-up version and not very successful. It carried approx. 60 rounds for the 17-pounder.

Churchill into Black Prince. The Churchill was itself underpowered and putting the same engine into a vehicle that was significantly heavier was clearly a mistake. A proposal was then made that after the initial batch of vehicles had been produced, Black Prince would be fitted with the Rolls Royce Meteor engine.

Six vehicles were built and the Tank Museum at Bovington has one in mint condition, while another has recently been recovered from Salisbury Plain. And, if rumour is correct, another is buried 'somewhere in Grantham'. The 17-pounder was eventually brought into the field of battle by mounting it on a Sherman tank and calling it the Firefly. This was in fact a very successful conversion and it was one of the very few pieces of specialized armour developed by the British in which the Americans were actually interested. However, being mounted onto a Sherman chassis it inherited all that vehicle's problems, such as thin armour and the ease with which it would 'brew up'. Also, there were never enough of them to go around which made them very precious assets and prime targets for Tigers and Panthers.

Whilst the Sherman, Cromwell and Comet were the backbone of the British armoured forces until the end of the war, the Black Prince project was still very much alive. It had been reported at the thirty-eighth meeting of the Tank Board (the department responsible for tank design) on 23 February 1944 that amongst all the other designs being worked on during those dark days, the final specification of A41, later to become famous as the Centurion, was accepted. The design of any new tank was still very much tied in with the outmoded designations that classed vehicles as infantry, cruiser, light and medium tanks. To that end, Centurion was classed as a heavy cruiser, whilst Churchill was an infantry tank.

Tests had proved that the minimum side armour needed to defeat the German 88mm (3.5in) gun was 4in (100mm), which would raise A41's weight to 50 tons (50,800kg). This was not considered advisable at this stage of development. Thus, as the next step forward from A41, investigations would start on the development of a vehicle with frontal armour of 6in (150mm) and a side belt of 4in. This new design was taken up in 1944 to be known as the A45 and this was to provide a vehicle to carry out the infantry role in support of Centurion, and we now see the first seeds of what would become FV 214 Conqueror.

Meanwhile, the Black Prince would not go away and at the meeting on 4 May 1944 of the Tank Board it was noted that Vauxhall (Black Prince design patents) was attempting to force the issue of orders for the tank. It was proposed that an order for 300 vehicles be placed, but the DRAC would not

Centurion Mk VII

Length	25ft 7in
Width	10ft 10in
Height	9ft 10in
Weight	114,245lb
Power	Rolls Royce Meteor V12 petrol 650bhp
Crew	4
Armament	105mm
Secondary armament	2 x .30 Browning machine guns
Armour	Max 5.98in Min 0.66in
Speed	21mph

Notes The first Centurions made it to Germany at the end of the war but were too late to see any fighting. Originally armed with a 17 pounder and 20mm Polsten cannon, it went to 20-pounder and .30 Browning before being fitted with probably one of the most famous tank guns ever produced, the 105mm. Introduction of this weapon was one of the causes for the demise of Conqueror. It served in many different variations with many variants, serving on long after Chieftain had replaced the gun tank. In the Gulf Centurion 165mm-armed AVRE served on with the Royal Engineers, but that was their swan song. Centurion is one of the most successful vehicles that Britain has produced, and even today they still serve in many countries.

agree to the production of the Bedford-engined vehicle, and he also saw the need for three variants as opposed to the one that was being offered. Although an order was finally placed, by the time of the invasion of Europe and with the end of the war looming cuts in production were discussed at the forty-third meeting of the Board, and it was decided that only twenty Black Prince per month would be built.

The Universal Tank

Pressure for a capital or universal tank to carry out all tasks was seen to emanate from General Montgomery's 21st Army Group which had produced a pamphlet for such a vehicle. In January 1945 it was announced that the Black Prince was running well on trials, and development of A45 was going well with the hull following the shape of A41 Centurion but with vertical sides and four suspension units per side. The prototype would be ready by mid 1946 weighing about 55 tons (55,880kg) and a top speed of 18mph (29km/h).

In February of 1945 Montgomery issued his memorandum on British Armour, stating a requirement for a capital tank around 45 tons (45,720kg) fitted with a dual-purpose gun and carrying 80 rounds of ammunition. Interest in the A43 Black Prince quickly waned, speeded by a damning report on the third prototype which was submitted on 22 March 1945. It is said that Major J. B. Dixon one of the trial officers, was summoned to the War Office to explain the offensive report; in fact, he had only produced a defect list on the vehicle and not the report. Finally, in May 1945 the Armoured Fighting Vehicle (AFV) schools were informed that Black Prince would not now be produced.

A great step forward was announced in 1946 when, at the insistence of many senior officers, including Field Marshal Montgomery, the artificial and constraining titles of infantry and cruiser tanks were abandoned, thus relieving designers of the many restrictions that these designations placed on them. This lifting would in turn lead to what we know today as the Main Battle Tank (MBT). At about this time the Tank Board was also dissolved and the grouping of vehicles was revised, with armoured vehicles becoming 'A' vehicles, and trucks and softskins 'B' vehicles. The newly

The FV200 series ARV/AVRE hull. The final shape of many of Conqueror's components can clearly be seen here. Notice the remote controlled .30 Browning in the armoured barbette on the front left of the superstructure. The Mk II Conqueror ARV bears a very strong resemblance to this vehicle. Tank Museum.

formed Fighting Vehicle Research and Development Establishment (FVRDE) at Chobham and Chertsey would now develop armoured vehicles.

In keeping with this policy, it was also announced what Britain's future types of AFV were to be. A45 had now become FV200. The decision had now been taken to make the FV200 series into a universal tank. This would, it was hoped, produce many different variants on a common hull and also save a great deal of money, a subject dear to politicians even in the late 1940s. Another reason for this decision was that investigations had shown that Centurion's hull design would not be able to take the increased armour and weapons fit that was envisaged for it to complete all of its tasks. There was also some doubt as to the adaptability of

Centurion's hull to take some of the specialist vehicles, of which twelve different types were planned including at least two AVREs (Armoured Vehicles Royal Engineers).

These would be numbered using the new system, with FV200 as the common hull and an all-up weight (depending on variant) of 35–60 tons (35,560–60,960kg). The following vehicles were envisaged:

- FV201 the Universal Tank
- FV202 AVRE (T)
- FV203 AVRE (L)
- FV204 Universal Flail
- FV205 SP Medium Anti-Tank Mounting
- FV206 SP Medium Artillery
- FV207 SP Heavy Artillery

Just to prove that anything can be made to float, here is an FV200 hull with the DD screen and equipment fitted ready to attempt to swim. Although records are vague it is reported that it was successfully floated. Notice the civilian numberplate on the front left mudguard. Tank Museum.

At last the British get it right, MkI Centurion in this configuration. The first six models were sent to Germany but were too late to fire a shot in anger. Notice the rolled plate turret soon changed to an all-cast one, the hatches for all-turret crew and the co-axial 20mm polsten cannon to the right of the 17-pounder. Tank Museum

- FV 208 Universal Bridgelayer
- FV209 Universal ARV
- FV210 Tractor Heavy Artillery
- FV211 Tractor Medium Artillery
- FV212 Assault Personnel Carrier.

The FV201

Thus at last the idea of a universal tank seemed to have borne fruit, with the FV201 to be the main gun tank of the FV200 series. By 1947 a lot of the groundwork had been completed, and members of the DRAC conference that year were shown the plans and given a briefing on progress during their visit to the FVRDE at Chobham.

The original A41 (Centurion) soft boat (mild steel) hull was rebuilt as a development vehicle for the FV200 series. It had been stripped down and a 15in (380mm) section inserted so as to make it as close as possible a representative of the FV200 hull

With the advantage of hindsight, one can see the first inkling of what was to be the eventual role for Conqueror, when during the 1948 DRAC conference, under the heading of Equipment Policy, it was stated, that 'there is an *essential* requirement for an heavily armed and armoured tank that will be capable of destroying from the front, any known or projected enemy tank beyond any range that they might be expected to attain.' At the same conference, the Director General of Fighting Vehicles was able to give this report:

FV201 is at the stage of having run 500–600 miles to test the running gear and suspension, it is hoped that the trials will be completed by 1951 and the vehicle ready to go into production in 1952. The design work on the DD [amphibious] variant is complete and we hope to have the first prototype by next year.

Also discussed were the relative merits of the Russian tank, JS3, which was to be the bogey tank for the West for many years, although here it seems to have been dismissed almost contemptuously. It was stated that it was 'an orthodox tank with

120mm of armour sloped at 55 degrees on the front of the hull, with the turret front having about 200mm'. It carried 28 rounds of main armament ammunition and at this time it was considered the equivalent of Centurion 3.

FV201 was a logical development of Centurion, incorporating a number of decisions taken by the War Office to implement short-term policy on the universal tank. It was accepted that these criteria could be met within the constraints of current technology. The universal tank would inevitably lead to compromises, for a tank fully adept in one role would not be so adept in another role. It was felt that with many components coming from Centurion the performance and reliability of these components would be more assured than if they came from a new design.

FV201 was meant originally to complement Centurion, although some intended it to be the replacement for it and for a while the vehicle laboured under the title of Super Centurion . The powers that be saw it as the ideal replacement vehicle for Centurion as it met the War Office criteria for the following reasons:

1) The reintroduction of the fifth crew man.
2) Increased ammunition load with greater access.
3) Increased armour protection.
4) Return of the bow machine gun.
5) Improved vision and sighting equipment.
6) Flame gun.
7) Better ventilation and electrical supply.
8) Livelier performance.
9) Easier conversion to the DD or dozer role.
10) Lower ground pressure.

These advantages increased the weight by 7 tons (7,112kg) and width by 23in (584mm).

The main armament was to be the 20-pounder, but having an improved performance over the gun fitted in Centurion III. It was calculated to be able to penetrate 240mm (9in) of homogeneous plate at 1,000yd (914m). Like Conqueror, it was to have for the period a very lavish and state-of-the-art fire-

JS3

Length	22ft 4in
Width	10ft 6in
Height	8ft 11in
Weight	101,963lb
Power	Model V-2IS V12 water-cooled diesel 520bhp
Crew	4
Armament	122mm
Secondary armament	1x 7.62mm co-ax 1x 12.7mm on turret
Armour	Max 5.19in Min 0.74in
Speed	23mph

Notes This was the main reason for the development of Conqueror. It is easy now with hindsight to examine the JS3 to see whether it is as fearsome as it was thought way back in the 1950s. When it first appeared in the Berlin victory parade in 1945 Western observers were stunned, for despite its large gun and good protection the vehicle weighed no more than the German Panzer and was almost as agile. However, this was at the expense of internal stowage and crew comfort. This made it an uncomfortable vehicle to fight, thus creating crew fatigue, the loader because of his cramped position and the size of the 122mm rounds so that at best he could only manage three rounds a minute loading. Not much good when you have a Conqueror that could manage six rounds a minute and Centurion even faster. It served with all the Warsaw Pact countries, but the only export customer was Egypt which bought about fifty. They came up against Israeli Centurions armed with the British 105mm in some of the early Arab–Israeli wars and were easily destroyed. The JS3 left service with the Russians in the early 1970s.

M103

Length	37ft 4in
Width	12ft 4in
Height	9ft 5in
Weight	125,000lb
Power	Continental AV 1790-5B V12 diesel 810bhp
Crew	5
Armament	120mm
Secondary armament	1x.30 Browning 1x .50 Browning
Armour	Max 7in Min 0.47in
Speed	21mph

Notes The M103 was the US equivalent of Conqueror armed with virtually the same weapon. It was also designed to provide support at long range. Interestingly, a crew of five, two of whom were loaders, served it and it carried only thirty-seven rounds of 120mm ammunition. It was introduced in 1952 with 200 being built, but the design was rushed and a vast number of modifications were required before the American Army would accept it. On the introduction of the British 105mm into the M48/60 series it was phased out, although the American Marines used a version called M103A1E1 based on three prototypes built in 1963 with many modifications including a new diesel engine. 1,553 vehicles were converted to this standard for the Marines. However, like Conqueror its time was up and it finally was withdrawn from service in 1973.

control system, which included a scanning device for the commander giving him 360 degrees of vision, a built-in rangefinder and a device that would automatically apply corrections to range and deflection caused by movement of the target and the tank itself. The cautionary point here is the use of the word 'devices', and one must ask the question how near to being operational were the devices or was it just a hopeful dream?

The inevitable question as to the capability of the vehicle to be up-gunned in the future produced answers that sounded the first hints on the death knell of the project. While it was certainly possible to up-gun the vehicle, it was found that if a gun bigger than the 20-pounder was fitted it would mean that the General Staff would have to be prepared to accept that a maximum of only thirty–thirty-five rounds could be carried. Also the bow machine gun would have to be removed, as would the fifth member of the crew in order to accommodate the larger ammunition. The loader would be required to handle the larger ammunition, which might be either fixed or split. Any up-armouring would therefore lead to a loss of performance that would not be acceptable, and also

the ability to carry the proposed DD gear and some of the proposed specialist attachments that had been planned was also in doubt as the present type of suspension would not be adequate.

Many other ideas were being sounded out, one of which was to build and install a gas turbine in an AFV. It was decided that the FV201 would be the ideal vehicle for this and a contract was given to C. A. Parsons of Newcastle to investigate the possibilities. The fruits of this research would be utilized in the FV214 programme, which would lead to Britain becoming the first country to power a major AFV with a gas turbine engine.

In his book on the history of the RTR *The Tanks*, the author Kenneth Macksey states that the abandonment of the FV201 was announced at the DRAC conference on 27 October 1948. It is interesting to note that we are only talking about the cancellation of the gun tank, as it was felt that the specialist versions could still be produced as they would still have a valuable supporting role to play.

The cancellation might well have been a subject for informal discussion, but the report for the 1948 conference contains no mention of it. However, it is known that the project was definitely being given

Not quite there, the A45 prototype, mounting the new turret for Centurion showing how much better shape the cast turret was. Notice again the use of a remote operated .30 machine gun on the front left track guard.

What all the panic was about: a JS3 in Germany. Notice how low and squat it appears, and the sharp angles on the glacis plate. Pity the poor loader working in such craped conditions.

serious consideration at about this period. Also under discussion at the 1948 conference was the armament for FV201 and the up-armouring and the penalties that we have seen that this would entail. It was also pointed out that there would be an increase in man hours for production of such a complex vehicle.

Throughout 1949 FV200 development carried on unabated until the new policy for armoured vehicles was raised in the Fighting Vehicle Division notes for October 1949. The reason given then for the cancellation was not purely due to the technical problems that had arisen, but a study carried out to find a tank with a gun that could penetrate the JS3 at a battle range. The 20-pounder that was to be fitted to FV201 was now not considered to be capable of this, partly due to inaccurate estimations of the frontal armour of the JS3. Originally the intelligence services had given the armour

protection for JS3 as 200mm (7.8in) thick, sloped at 45 degrees. Penetration of the 20-pounder firing from 1,000yds (914m) was only 188mm (7.3in) reducing to 166mm (6.5in) at 2,000yd (1,830m). This all sounds very familiar for it would seem that the British had yet again fallen into the trap of reliance on a single weapon (the 20-pounder) which now seemed not to be equal to the task.

As a result, the War of Office became gripped by an almost panic mentality for it seemed that the Russians fielding the JS3 could roam the battlefield with total impunity, just as the Germans had with the Tiger during World War II. (It was much later discovered by intelligence and examination of the real vehicle that the armour on JS3 was not as great as had been estimated!)

With FV201 now well and truly dead, the search was on for a new vehicle. It was decided that the minimum calibre of weapon to be fitted would be

120mm (4.7in), although calibres of 146mm (5.7in) and 180mm (7in) were looked at. In the end, only three FV201s were built and these were eventually used in the development of Conqueror. The FV201 was 25ft long, 13ft wide (7.5m x 4m) with a top speed of 19mph (30km/h) from its 800bhp Meteor fuel-injected engine, which gave it a range of about 110 miles (177km). The hull gunner's machine gun was uniquely situated not in the hull but in a remote-controlled armoured mounting on the front left wing; this was designed to leave space in the hull for the fitting of the flame gun if required.

The driver was provided with three periscopes for closed-down driving, as against two for Centurion. The vehicle ran on eight small road wheels per side, but in a radical departure from traditional British design they were of a resilient rim type consisting of a steel outer tyre with the rubber encased inside. Suspension was of the Horstman type similar to Centurion, in which movement of the axle arms compressed horizontal springs. Four units were fitted each side. The turret was basically the same as fitted to Centurion, but was provided with an adapter ring to allow for the greater width of the vehicle; stowage was provided for seventy-five 20-pounder rounds.

By October 1949, however, the second prototype was running with the flame equipment fitted. Although by this time the decision to cancel FV201 had been made, it was decided to carry out flame trials with it with a view to possible fitting of the equipment to Centurion. It had already been decided that FV214 was not to have a flame capability. In April 1950 the flame equipment was removed and the vehicle was ballasted to simulate the expected weight of Conqueror.

Even before its cancellation, 1949 had proved to be a bad year for the FV201 project as various problems had started to surface. The first of these was the rather belated discovery that the flail variant of FV201 needed a hull some several inches longer to accommodate the extra gearbox required to drive the flail drum. In view of this it was decided that the flail would go ahead as a separate project, although some thought had been given to providing

a 1,000hp secondary engine to drive the flail drum. In the end, the whole project was cancelled in April 1949. The next blow was the discovery that the DD tank would not fit into the standard Mk VIII landing craft, and it was projected that the modified landing craft would not be available for some considerable time. Almost as an afterthought, it was found that the ill-fated flail tank would not fit either.

So the end came in April 1949, for all of the reasons noted above. It was also felt that by the time that FV201 came into service, it would be so far behind anything that a potential enemy would be able to field that it would be of no use whatever. It was also decided that some of the specialized variants could be based on redundant or obsolete hulls such as Churchill and early Centurions. The resulting lack of mobility (in the Churchill's case) would be acceptable as a cost-saving measure.

The result of all this was the adoption of Centurion to become the main tank of the Royal Armoured Corps, with FV201 being redesigned as a long-range heavy tank killer to support Centurion. This decision was taken whilst still stating the need for a long-range, large-calibre equipped tank to support Centurion.

As we have seen, the vehicle that was responsible for this upset was the JS3. With its well-angled hull, low profile and 122mm (4.8in) gun, it was feared the JS3 would be able to defeat Centurion before Centurion could get into range to be able to defeat it. To that end, the RAC asked for a tank with better armour and a large calibre gun that could defeat JS3 at long ranges. Thus in that requirement the remarks made in DRAC's conference of 1948 had at last borne fruit.

However, there were still problems to be overcome, not least that having decided on the calibre of 120mm (4.7in) for the new tank's gun, Britain did not have such a weapon nor was one under development. The only existing 120mm belonged to the USA in the shape of their T53 gun derived from an anti-aircraft weapon, which would need many modifications before it was ready to fit into a tank. There was no APDS (armour-piercing discarding sabot) round for it either, and due to this modification requirement the Ministry of Supply stated that it could only produce a tank mounting this weapon in January 1954 at the earliest.

The hull chosen to mount the new weapon was to be that of the FV201, although first indications showed that unless the hull was modified to a great extent the driver would be forced to enter and exit via the turret. However, by removing the power take off and all the flame thrower internal fittings it was found that the new turret could be fitted onto an FV201 hull. The hull carrying the new turret would be designated as FV214.

However, as it was known that the turret could not be ready until at least January 1954 it was felt that production should go ahead with the hulls. This raised several options on how these could best be used:

- Place weight on the hull to simulate all-up weight.
- Mount a Centurion III turret on the hull weighted to represent the weight of the new turret.
- A compromise between the above.

The final answer was for the hull to be fitted with a Centurion turret and the resulting vehicle would be known as FV221. Some hulls were fitted with weights sometimes known as a Windsor turret (one vehicle so fitted survives to this day in working order). To fit the Centurion turret to the FV201 an adapter ring was required, but apart from that the turret was the same as for a production Centurion gun tank. By doing this, the end user at last could have experience in handling a large vehicle such as the FV214.

A wooden frame mock-up of what the Conqueror turret may have looked like, this would enable designers to see whether the projected design was feasible and where various components could be situated. Tank Museum.

The official requirement was proposed in June 1949 and it was decided to go ahead and produce the new vehicle to be known as the FV214 heavy gun tank no. 1. However, things did not go well at first for when it came to placing the orders for the new tank, these orders were amended, cancelled and amended yet again. In September 1952 it was decided to order 250 vehicles over the next three years, but even in March of the following year there was still great confusion concerning these orders. In addition, a true representative mock-up had still not been seen, nor had the RAC set its seal of approval on the project. With all this confusion it is surprising that the vehicle ever saw the light of day.

At the DRAC conference of November 1949 a proposal was forwarded for FV214 to mount a two-man turret. This found favour in some quarters as it would save weight, present a better ballistic shape and, possibly the main reason for its popularity, it would save money. Against this would have to be set the increased workload that it would have meant for the crew. The two-man turret school of thought then proposed that an automatic rammer should be fitted to ease the loader's job, and they also envisaged a second crew for the vehicle, who could carry out all the normal maintenance jobs at night while the operational crew slept (which the Americans had tried without great success). Faced with this, it is not surprising that the two-man turret idea was allowed to die quietly.

At the end of the same conference the main features of the vehicle had at last emerged. It was to carry 35 rounds of split-case type ammunition and it was to be armed with a 120mm gun based on an American anti-aircraft weapon. The turret would have a turret ring of 80in (2030mm) and weigh 18 tons (18,288kg); this was 6in (152mm) wider and 5 tons (5,080kg) heavier than Centurion. No stabilizer system was to be fitted but power control for traverse and elevation would be provided. No

The shape is getting there. This model is clad in metal plates, and could well be the mock-up to show what the turret with two men in the FCT would look like. Tank Museum.

integrated fire-control system was to be fitted, although the commander would be provided with an RCP (Reflector Cum Periscope) sight and an optical range finder.

The Director General of Fighting Vehicles then addressed the conference on the current state of AFV development. The FV214 heavy gun tank and FV221 medium gun tank were under development, and the basic details of FV214 were a vehicle weighing 63 tons (64,000kg) with a crew of four housed in a traditional layout of driver and turret crew. The main gun was to be a 120mm weapon and secondary armament would be 2 x 30 Browning machine guns. Due to the size of the 120mm ammunition it would be of the split-type projectile and brass case so approximately only thirty-five rounds could be carried. A Rolls Royce Meteor petrol-injected engine

developing 800bhp would drive it; an auxiliary generator engine was to be fitted to the supply power without the need to run the main engine.

The FV221 would be identical in respect of engine, running gear and suspension units – differing only in the fitting of the Centurion turret, this would give the user time to get used to the bulk of the new vehicle. The most important feature of the FV221 was its ability to be converted into an FV214 once the turrets were available, and we shall see later how this in fact happened.

It was also stated that there would be no requirement for internal flame fitting for either vehicle, but both had to be capable of mounting a dozer blade. Also to be produced was a specialist ARV to cope with the weight of the heavy tank. The main aim of the heavy gun tank programme was

FV221 Caernarvon pictured on Bovington Heath. The final hull shape for Conqueror is now there but to give troops experience with such a large vehicle a Centurion III turret was fitted till the Conqueror turrets were ready. Notice the Centurion turret now armed with the first version of the 20-pounder gun. Tank Museum.

Panic measures. The one and only model of Conway. This was a War Office idea to get the 120mm gun to the troops as soon as possible. It consisted of a Centurion III hull with a large fabricated high side turret carrying the 120mm gun. One problem associated with Conway was that it was not recommended to fire the gun whilst over either side, as there was a real fear of the vehicle falling over. Only one was built and can be seen at Bovington Tank Museum. Tank Museum.

that of getting the vehicle into service in the shortest possible time. This was not an easy task and, as we shall see, it was complicated almost daily.

By December 1955 it was reported that production was slow due to additional modifications required as a result of the trials that had been conducted in Germany and other locations. In 1957 it was decided that the order should be reduced further and only 150 vehicles bought, although this was then changed to 180. In the end, only 152 true Conquerors were actually built, and seven FV221, now known as Caernarvons, were converted to the latest standards at the end of Dalmuir's Conqueror production.

Even with all the planning under way for two

new vehicles that could destroy the JS3 and hopefully any other new Russian vehicles, the War Office was still anxious. It required a counter to the JS3 to be in service sooner than later in the fifties, the predicted date in service of the FV214. As a result, the FV4004 project was born. This consisted of a Centurion III hull with a large slab-sided turret designed by, of all companies, the Auster Light Aircraft Co. of Rearsby, Leicestershire, and built by Chubb's of Wolverhampton. The whole vehicle was assembled at ROF Barnbow in Leeds.

The weapon that was picked to arm the vehicle, now known as Conway, was the same American gun that would be destined for Conqueror – the L1A1 120mm. There were severe problems with the design as a weight limit of 50 tons (50,800 kg) had been imposed. In order to encompass this restriction and also mount the gun high enough, the turret had to be of a great height. This in turn raised the centre of gravity to an alarming extent. It also created major problems if the vehicle was ever to be transported by road or rail.

By fitting the turret onto a Centurion hull the turret ring was smaller than that proposed for the FV214, so an adapter ring was required. This produced a vehicle with only 5 degrees depression and 10 degrees elevation, not much better than some of the contemporary Russian tanks. Ammunition load was only twenty rounds mixed of APDS/HESH with eleven being ready rounds.

Only one vehicle was actually built, with full production due to commence in 1952. However, it was realized that this was not the vehicle to answer the threat of the JS3, and although trials continued so that the design could swiftly be resurrected if the need ever arose, the project was officially cancelled in December 1952. The only vehicle built, 07 BA 67, survives to this day in the Tank Museum at Bovington. This project was not the only panic measure that was undertaken to counter the JS3, and we shall deal with those in a later chapter.

We can now see that tank designers did not have an easy time trying to get their vehicles into production, and as the next Chapter will reveal the production path was also fraught with setbacks. In fact, there were usually so many changes and cancellations that one wonders how anything ever actually happened.

2 Production

THE FV214 AND FV221

As we have already seen, the Royal Armoured Corps by the middle of 1948 was in rather a quandary as to what vehicle to develop to combat the JS3, especially given the cancellation of the FV201 gun tank part of the FV200 series (although the variants on this chassis were still being developed). It was recognized that a large gun, preferably of 120mm, must be mounted on a vehicle and produced with the utmost speed. The only vehicle that could mount such a large calibre weapon was the hull of the cancelled FV200, so the decision was taken to utilize that hull and running gear and design a new turret to mount the 120mm gun. The new vehicle was known as the FV214. On the basis of this proposal the following timetable was suggested:

- April 1950 – FV221 design complete and order placed by War Office, along with tooling up and ordering of materials.
- September 1951 – FV 214 prototype trials commence.
- March 1952 – FV214 designs sealed.
- April 1952 – first FV221 off production line.
- January 1954 – first FV214 off production line.

However, as a result of discussions it was felt that full production of the new tank could not be initiated without user trials. It was 'asked if it would be possible to produce for troop trial purposes a small number of the proposed FV221 fitted with a Centurion III turret.'

It was found that twenty such vehicles could be produced, with the first being delivered probably about April 1952. This would produce yet more delay in the production of FV214, with the minimum of at least twelve months being expected, although the reality was more likely to be eighteen months. This was, however, felt to be acceptable and plans were made for the project to go ahead.

The twenty models to be produced for the troop trials were to be built at the Royal Ordnance Factory at Barnbow in Leeds. A whole production line was to be created there which would ultimately produce eight to ten FV221 or FV214 per month. With the ROF using some existing jigs and tooling from the Centurion line, the cost to tool one complete line would be in the region of £125,000, with the cost of the twenty FV221s coming to £1,400,000, or £70,000 each.

The War Office assumed that troop trials would probably last for eighteen months after the delivery of the first vehicle. In view of that timescale it was decided that no order for FV214 would be placed until the end of the trials. The timetable now resembled something akin to this:

- April 1950 – Order placed for twenty FV221 for troop trials.
- September 1951 – FV214 prototype trial begins.
- March 1952 – FV214 production design sealed.
- April 1952 – First model of FV221 from production line.
- April 1953 – First twenty production models of FV221 delivered.
- October 1953 – troop trials of FV221 complete and order for FV214 placed.
- June 1955 – First production model of FV214 off the production line.

It would seem right to take a few moments to explain why the requirement for troop trials was so important. Troop trials were, and still are, a very important part of vehicle development. They allow the user to have hands-on experience of what might become his main piece of equipment for many years. It can also stop a project dead in its tracks. In my time on Chieftain we ran many trials even though the vehicle was in full service and managed either to stop or at least change many dubious ideas that were put forward by well-intentioned designers who unfortunately never got to see the vehicle until it was too late. Troop trials in this case were important, due to the pressure on the FV214 not to fail.

The final decision as to which plan would be accepted by the War Office was dependent on whether it would accept a delay of eighteen months getting the FV214 in the field to the troops with a resulting loss of eighteen months' production. The running gear and hull of FV221 and FV214 would not be radically different from the basic FV200 series, of which prototypes were now conducting automotive trials. There were no major ground-breaking advances in the construction of either vehicle, more a series of logical follow-on steps from the Centurion.

It was felt that the FV221 would be a better vehicle than Centurion III, even though it was to mount the same weapon, and it had the added advantage that it could quite easily be converted into an FV214 when that vehicle's turrets became available. It was suggested around this time that approximately 1,830 FV214s would be required, of which 936 would be needed by the actual RAC Regiments and the rest for training and trials. This number is somewhat optimistic, as it would have meant a very high number of vehicles not being gainfully employed.

During March 1950 the Director of Weapons and Development forwarded the War Office specification for what was then known as the British heavy gun tank no. 1 FV214.

At first it seemed as though the vehicle was to follow the existing, and what had almost become traditional, layout of British tanks, but the RAC was in for a shock. The main characteristics of the vehicle were to be follows:

- Should not weigh more than 150,000lb.
- Length to be as short as possible.
- Width must not exceed 13ft (4m).
- Height must not exceed 10ft (3m).
- Must be transportable by rail in Europe.

The Tortoise

The A39 Tortoise was a major British triumph of common sense over reality. It was designed as an assault tank in 1942 and as such it mounted the 3.7in anti-aircraft gun. This weapon, if mounted in a proper tank, would have been a world-beater. It could destroy anything on the battlefield during WW II. However, it was mounted in Tortoise, and so never reached its true potential.

Tortoise was 23ft 9in long with a fixed superstructure carrying the weapon. It had armour 8.86in thick at its maximum and 1.38 minimum. Its total weight was 174,720lb. Powered by a Rolls Royce Meteor 12-cylinder petrol engine developing 600hp gave it a top speed of 12mph.

If it had made it to the battlefield it would have been no more than a slow moving pillbox. For secondary armament it was equipped with three Besa machine guns, two in a commander's turret with the third mounted in the hull front. The tank transporters of the day would have struggled to move it. The project was not pushed very hard and the six prototypes were not completed till 1947. One, or possibly two, were sent to Germany for mobility trials and surprisingly proved fairly agile although slow. The aim of this was to gather sufficient data in case the need ever arose to build a super-heavy tank again. Their fate is almost predictable, one remains today in the Tank Museum at Bovington while the other five have been destroyed as hard targets, although one did languish behind the Tank Museum until the mid-1960s when it was despatched to Lulworth.

- Main armament of 120mm.
- Secondary armament of two machine guns (it was hoped that these would be the new British-developed tank machine gun, but this was cancelled so .30 Browning were used instead).
- Smoke grenade dischargers were to be fitted.
- Empty cases would be automatically ejected from the turret.
- Rate of fire was expected to be six rounds in the first minute followed by three rounds in subsequent minutes.
- Normal radios of the time to be fitted.
- Night-fighting equipment, i.e. infrared, was desirable.
- Auxiliary generator to be fitted.
- Assisted loading.

So far, the specifications all seemed pretty normal, but the shock was still to come.

As we saw in the previous chapter, many ideas had been discussed as to the eventual shape and type of turret to be employed on FV214. One suggestion had been for a two-man turret, which would have both provided a very good ballistic-shaped turret and saved the Treasury money. The logistical load placed on the two remaining crew members, however, would have been too much and for that and other reasons this idea was not taken up. Since then, a lot of thought had been given to the eventual design. It was to be immune over a frontal arc of 60 degrees from a 100mm (4in) weapon with about 13in (330mm) frontal armour and 7in (178mm) on the sides. A co-axial machine gun was to be fitted with a second mounted in the sub-turret. This is where the big change to the normal layout occurred. It was felt that it would be desirable to place both the gunner and commander in a sub-turret mounted in the bustle of the main turret, with the commander on the right and the gunner on the left. This was to enable either of them to operate the cross-turret rangefinder, which was deemed necessary to the vehicle to give it a first-round hit probability of 80% at a range of 2,000yd (1,830m). Also fitted to the sub-turret was all the fire-control equipment, which would be operated independently of the main turret.

The reasons that this turret was the better choice of design were:

- It was overall a better shape ballistically.
- Its unique layout enabled the range-finding equipment to be used without disturbing the layout of the main gun.
- It gave up more turret space for main gun ammunition.
- It was expected that engagement times could be cut drastically.
- It provided a full turret fighting capacity if one member was injured by allowing either commander or gunner to fire the weapons, with one replacing the loader if required.

The War Office did also list its disadvantages, but these were very few:

- The fire-control equipment was far more complicated than normal, and far more so than an equivalent Russian tank.
- The commander had very restricted vision when fully closed down.

The response from the RAC centre was swift and to the point, stating that the proposals had been investigated and discussed and a unanimous decision to reject them had been reached. Part of the letter from HQ RAC to the Under Secretary of State at the War Office outlining the reasons is reproduced here:

It is difficult to see what the advantages were of having two men in the fire-control turret if they were unable to perform separate functions. Once the main turret was brought into the line-up position the fire-control turret must remain fixed to the main turret. This immediately restricted the commander's actions and made one man redundant. There would be occasions when there would be a need to scan the whole of the 360 degree spectrum, or fire the commander's machine gun or range to a new target. With the proposed layout this was not feasible.

However, the RAC centre did give credit were it was due and made the point that some features were quite desirable, such as the ability to range to a target without moving the main gun (useful if fully camouflaged up in a hide) and to make the main armament follow the same line as predicted by the range finder.

In view of these comments, the RAC asked for a layout:

- With only the commander in the turret and he should have at hand the facility to override the gunner's firing and power controls.
- That would be able to locate and range onto targets anywhere in a 360-degrees circle.
- That would leave the gunner to complete the fine laying and actual firing of the gun. He should also be located in the conventional gunner's crew position, which would still allow the designers to produce the ballistic shape that was required.

In the end, this is virtually the layout that was adopted for the FV214, although at this stage it still had all the indications of facing a very difficult birth. Matters were also not helped by the various conflicting orders on vehicle quantities that emanated from the War Office. It had been planned that only twenty FV221 vehicles were to be produced, but further discussion somewhere in a magical kingdom decided that the number would be increased to 160, with sixty being built in 1952–53 and 100 in 1953–54.

By October 1950 it had been realized that the increase had not taken into account the latest instructions for accelerated production of FV214. It was then proposed that after sixty FV221 had been built production could then change to FV214, giving a production of 100 FV214 in 1953–54 which would replace the original 100 FV221.

To get Conqueror into production therefore seemed as though it was going to be a major operation, for although the design had at last been finalized the placing of orders for vehicles was at the best haphazard. One can only guess at the feelings of the ROF management as the orders changed almost daily. In 1953–54, eight vehicles were ordered, for 1954–55 180, for 1955–56 192, and for 1956–57 192. The final orders after all the confusion amounted to 180 vehicles.

In June 1951 Vickers reported that the three FV221 prototypes that they were producing were on schedule and it was hoped to have one running by September 1951. This was first put back to October 1951 then December 1951. By now, the final shape of the FV214 turret had been decided on – it was to be produced from a one-piece casting, although alternative methods had been looked at.

While all this was taking place, the fitting of a 180mm gun in an armoured vehicle was still being sounded out. While some claimed that a 20-pounder was the largest that could be mounted, it was pointed out the USA had already mounted a 155mm gun into a turreted tank in the shape of the T30 in 1944. This all took valuable time and resources away from the FV214 project. Britain's 120mm guns had now been standardized, from the ammunition point of view at least, with the American T122 gun, the modified 120mm gun fitted to the prototype tank that later became the M103. By late October 1950 the mock-up FV221 hull with internal fittings was almost complete and work continued with manufacture of the prototype.

The date of December 1951 was also the target date for the first prototype FV214. The first turret had been successfully cast and patterns for the fire-control turret were nearly ready. Also by now proof firing of the gun had taken place, so at last it looked as if the new vehicles were making headway. It was decided to mount the 180mm gun on a Centurion hull, calling it FV4005 with a second using FV200 components known as FV215b.

Vickers reported on 31 December that the first FV221 prototype was ready except for fitting the electrical components, but the non-arrival of these components put back the date for commencing road trials. By March 1952 Vickers were able to report that the first prototype FV221 had completed its trials and was awaiting a turret and gun before being despatched. The Fighting Vehicles Division report for April 1952 no. 330 stated that the first

FV221 had completed 400 miles (644km) and was now having its Centurion turret removed and replaced with a superstructure designed to make the all-up weight near the 65 tons (66,040kg) of the production FV214. Also, the second prototype was complete and had just started its test mileage.

Four prototypes of the FV214 turrets had been cast; of these, one was due to be delivered to the second FV221 prototype when it arrived at FVDE. The gun, fire-control equipment and fire-control turret were to be fitted as and when they became available. This would then allow investigation to be carried out into the various fire-control systems and would further their development. Another of the turrets was to be used for defensive firing trials, which it was hoped would confirm the protection forecast for the turret. The remaining turrets would then be fitted to FV221 prototypes no. 3 and 4. Finally, a further FV214 hull was being produced for firing trials and eventually the second prototype turret would be fitted to it.

To complicate matters, the British were bound by a tripartite treaty to help develop a 150mm gun, and it was suggested that the advantages of mounting it on a light hull should now be looked at. However, it was felt that it would be disastrous for the FV214 if doubts were raised at this late stage; wiser heads appear to have prevailed and FV214 survived. By June 1952 the first main armament mounting had been fitted into an FV214 turret and it had now been delivered to Chobham.

The FV214, however, was still under considerable threat, not least from the other two services (nothing new there) for the cost of it. The Secretary of State held a meeting on 12 September 1952 to discuss the future of the vehicle and any alternatives. These were possibly the guided missile expected to reach fruition in five to six years' time; a liquid propellant gun also maybe in five to six years' time or a 120mm-armed Centurion. The first were too far away and the Centurion 120mm (Conway) was as we have seen, a large, bulky vehicle and not at all a satisfactory tank. It was estimated that at least two years would be needed to develop a lower silhouette for an 120mm-armed

Centurion.

Thus it was decided that there was a need for the 120mm to make it to the battlefield now, and the only vehicle that could do that at present was the FV214. Apart from sound tactical reasons for producing the FV214 it was also thought that it would serve as a morale booster to the troops. Finally it was agreed that the order for 250 FV214 was to be placed and Conway was to be cancelled. While all this in-fighting was going on, ways were being discussed to employ the FV214 within units, but this was something that was never resolved satisfactorily even until the last vehicle left active service. Of this we shall see more in a later chapter. To make matters even more confused, an order for 160 medium gun tanks no. 1 Caernarvon had been placed. When this vehicle had first been proposed in June 1949, it was intended that twenty, then forty and finally 160 vehicles would be built. However, by March 1953 the order had been reduced to ten vehicles.

CAERNARVON AND CONQUEROR

By now, the vehicles were becoming known by their issued names – FV221 was to be known as Caernarvon and FV214 to be known as Conqueror. As we have seen, the Caernarvon's place in the Conqueror story was due to the fact that once it had been decided to build a vehicle as large as the FV214, it was accepted that the RAC had no experience of operating a vehicle of that size. So Caernarvon was created in order to provide the future user with experience in the handling and logistics of large AFVs.

We have seen how both Conqueror and Caernarvon had to fight many battles before seeing the light of day, but for the most unusual attack Caernarvon must win hands down. Buried in the Public Record Archives is a letter from the town clerk of Caernarvon pointing out that some people, including the town clerk, were said to be very offended that the name of the town had been used without their agreement for the Army's new tank.

As noted above, Caernarvon was never meant to be anything more than a test bed for the user to obtain experience of operating a large, heavy AFV, and only ten vehicles were built. They were originally due to be issued out with two to BAOR, two to MELF, two to 4/7DG and one to the RAC Centre. In the end the allocation was as follows: 07 BA 77 and 07 BA 72 were sent to the RAC Centre at Bovington; the 8th Royal Tank Regiment received 07 BA 71; 07 BA 76 went to BAOR; 07 BA 74 and 07 BA 75 went to the 14/20th Hussars and took part in the hot weather trials as part of Middle East Land forces; 07 BA 73 was sent to the MTDE; and 07 BA 68, 07 BA 69 and 07 BA 70 remained at the FVRDE at Chertsey for further evaluation. One of the Chertsey vehicles has a small claim to fame in that 07 BA 70 was the vehicle that was fitted with the Parsons gas turbine and ran quite successfully with it for some time and at least twenty years ahead of the M1 Abrams! Out of these ten Caernarvons, seven were returned to ROF Dalmuir, which had become the main building centre for Conqueror outside Glasgow, after all the trials had been completed. They were then rebuilt to current standards and issued as Conqueror Mk2/1/H.

No complete Caernarvons are known to have survived to the present time, although at least three of the rebuilt vehicles exist in various states of preservation. We will look at their fate in a later chapter. The nearest that one can get to seeing a Caernarvon today is the Tank Museum's Conqueror that is located at the Imperial War Museum's vehicle collection at Duxford. This vehicle, 40 BA 81, is fitted with the ballasted turret seen on some of the Caernarvons to simulate the all-up weight of the production turret. The location of the turret is a mystery, but more than likely it has found itself on some anti-tank range being slowly destroyed. Looking at the vehicle, one will get an idea of how Caernarvon must have looked. It is hoped that the military wing of Duxford will eventually be able to find a surplus turret from a Centurion so that at last we may have a running replica of Caernarvon.

Bovington Tank Museum has a surviving Caernarvon hull. It is situated by the track used for demonstrations in the summer. The sad thing about this hull is that the Tank Museum seems to have lost a wonderful chance to promote a British first, for the hull belongs to Caernarvon 07 BA 70, the world's first gas-turbine-powered military vehicle; instead, the hull has been turned into a commentary box painted in a pseudo-camouflage paint scheme. Yet inside the museum is a gas turbine as used in the trials, which, although it is an amalgam of both engines, could have been on display next to the hull for posterity.

The acceptance meeting of February 1953 was at last shown a full-size hull fitted with a mock-up of the turret, and production was recommended at twenty vehicles for the period 1953–54. These were to be the troop trials vehicles, and by June 1953 work had started on these. In July 1955 the vehicles had arrived in BAOR (the first in April) after completing full-scale gunnery trials in the UK. A twenty-first vehicle was sent out in late April 1956, which was 40 BA 79 fitted with disc brakes as part of a trial within a trial.

The vehicles were issued to the various regiments taking part in the troop trials, but as there were only twenty-one vehicles available no one really received their full entitlement. This posed no great problem to the trials themselves, but it would

07 BA 70 being used as a dynamometer test vehicle at Christchurch after use as a test bed for the gas-turbine project. Note that it now carried the vehicle registration of 99 SP 46. Also of interest is the fact that it is fitted with tracks from a Chieftain MBT.

have given the participating units valuable experience in the logistic problems that they may have had to face on the introduction of the new tank if more numbers had been available. In the end, one unit had nine vehicles, another five with 40 BA 79 to follow once it had had its disc brakes fitted, and two other units had three each.

On the completion of the trials, all the vehicles were returned to ROF Dalmuir where they were fully stripped down and inspected. Seven were then rebuilt incorporating all the latest modifications and issued out to the RAC regiments, giving whoever received them the best Conqueror*s* produced.

PRODUCTION BEGINS

The main centre of production for Conqueror was based at the Royal Ordnance Factory at Dalmuir on the outskirts of Glasgow, with Leeds and Newcastle playing a smaller role. The major construction work that made Conqueror different from previous British tanks was the very large casting required for the turret. Possibly only the cast hull for the Tortoise which was developed at the end of the war had posed such problems before. The responsibility for producing the castings was entrusted to the firms of William Beardsmore and English Steel. All

the other components that had been sub-contracted would arrive at Dalmuir for final assembly and testing before being issued to the Army. The cost of a vehicle in 1952 was £30,032; this had risen to £47,904 in 1953 and if the contract for the final batch of vehicles had actually been taken up then the cost would have risen to £68,000. This is one of the inescapable problems in tank designing, that the cost never goes down and today a Challenger II would cost around £2.5m.

Production Problems

Like all production lines, nothing ever runs smoothly and Conqueror's was no exception. Throughout its production life it was plagued with problems, some large but inexcusable whilst others were very minor but were the sort that one would expect on a production line with a brand new vehicle. Add to all this the constant list of modifications that seemed to flow endlessly from the War Office and the problems with the trades unions, and it is almost a miracle that the vehicle escaped from the factory and made it into service with the regiments.

One of the very first problems that appeared was due to the method used to construct the suspension units. The designers had decided to use the same

Conqueror Mk I and Mk II

Length	38ft
Width	13ft 1in
Height	11ft
Weight	65 tons
Power	M120 12-cylinder V-injected petrol engine 801bhp
Crew	4
Armament	120mm rifled gun
Secondary armament	2x.30 Browning machine guns
Armour	max 6in min 1⅛in
Speed	21.5mph
Rounds	30

Notes Both marks of FV214 Conqueror gun tank were virtually identical with only small details giving the differences between marks away. Both carried the same fit of weapons and ammunition.

A newly completed Mk II Conqueror 41 BA 53 taken after its completion at the Royal Ordnance Factory at Dalmuir near Glasgow. Note the absence of either set of Bazooka plates and the commander's hatch locked in the open umbrella position.

style of Horstman suspension as used on the Centurion (and later Chieftain). The problem arose because it was decided that the units for Conqueror were to be cast in one piece as opposed to those for Centurion, which were fabricated and welded together. The first sign of trouble was noted after the delivery of the first fifteen vehicles, when it became apparent that cracks were appearing in the suspension units after only a very low mileage had been clocked up. The first steps taken were to inspect *all* units, including those fitted and issued, all spares and all tanks still on the production line. The problem was eventually traced to a missing symbol denoting the grade of steel to be used that had been omitted from the drawings given to the manufacturer of the units. The remedy was that *every* unit made so far had to be replaced and of course this put back production dates that were already falling behind.

Another major problem that occurred was in the failure of the petrol tanks after about five miles' driving. This, as can be imagined, was potentially dangerous, as the last thing the crew would need would be for gallons of petrol to be sloshing about in the confined hot spaces of the engine compartment. This was traced to changes to the specifications that were different to those tendered

by the company; the company concerned replaced all fuel tanks, but with the result that production was put back even further.

Whilst the above problems are representative of the sort that can befall any production line, the one problem that showed that the design team had not entirely lost its sense of humour was the awarding, after several trials, of the contract to produce the rangefinder for the Fire Control Turret to the Admiralty Research Department. The only reason that anyone can think of for the contract going there was that someone must have decided that as the Royal Navy had used rangefinders in its capital warships, ergo they must be a fount of knowledge. Unfortunately it did not quite work out that way. Even more amazing was the fact that literally just down the road from ROF Dalmuir was the optical firm of Barr and Stroud who were well versed in vehicle optics, and still serve the Army well in the field of optronics to this day.

The type of rangefinder that had been chosen was the coincidence type where the operator had to line up a split image, rather like the viewfinder in an early Rangefinder camera. This system was picked in preference to the American system of stereoscopic rangefinding after intensive trials with recruits at the Gunnery School at Lulworth Camp. It soon became obvious that the coincidence type was by far the easier system to use; also most people could use it whereas a lot of people had problems trying to adjust their eyesight to the stereoscopic system.

However, problems soon arose with trying to retain coincidence both in setting the rangefinder's zero and when using it to range, and so rather belatedly Barr and Stroud were called in to help. One recorded comment by them on the instrument produced so far was that 'as a rangefinder it makes a really useful thermometer.' This was due to the fact that in the majority the cases the loss of coincidence could be attributed to a rapid temperature change when the armoured shutters on the fire-control turret, which protected the heads of the rangefinder, were opened and the heads were exposed to outside temperatures. Barr and Stroud pointed out that most of the principles used by the Admiralty were at the best prehistoric and did not take account of certain more up-to-date principles that had been developed by Barr and Stroud. These principles were not patented to Barr and Stroud so were freely available to any company that wished to make use of them.

Barr and Stroud made many improvements to the design, and eventually produced a working model that was put into production. Research carried on until they came up with a package that would have made the rangefinder foolproof, but these would not be available to be embodied until 1958 and by then the General Staff had already taken the decision to phase out Conqueror.

The complex and very lavish layout of the fire-control system designed for Conqueror came years before the age of solid-state electronics, hi-tech and advanced fire-control computers, which meant that there was always going to be a high chance of problems with the system. One that was never cured was that after the FCT and main turrets had come to halt after a line-up action had taken place, both turrets would oscillate a few degrees either side of the centre line, a feature that was not going to help in accurate laying or observation. DRAC in the end was forced to accept a modified system in order to

get the vehicle into service as units were starting to get impatient for their new vehicles. This decision robbed Conqueror's fire-control system the chance of ever being rectified and giving the performance of which it would undoubtedly have been capable.

However, if you were to ask any Conqueror crewman today what fault they can remember causing the most problems and which should have been cured at the production stage if not even earlier, the answer would probably be, 'the Mollins ejector gear'.

This equipment was designed as an absolute must, as an aid for the loader in keeping the turret clear of spent 120mm brass cases. Previously, ideas for clearing the spent brass case from the turret had been based on the gun returning to a set elevation and the case being ejected through a hatch in the turret. However, that idea was deemed to be too complicated and in addition it meant breaking the lay of the gun too much, with the penalty that the gunner might not take the same point of aim when the gun returned to its original lay.

The Mollins gear operated on the principle of the empty case landing on a plate, which caused a switch to be closed and a hoist activated which would take the case to a hatch in the turret wall. This would automatically open and the case would be ejected outside. The system as designed was to be activated during firing, when the empty case

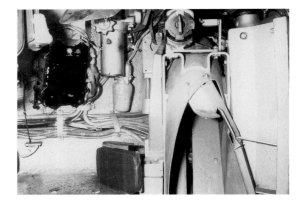

Showing the ejection chute of the Mollins ejector gear with the gunner's backrest to the right of it.

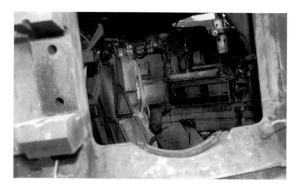

This picture, taken through the aperture for the main armament, shows the lower and upper portions of the case ejection chute of the Mollins gear.

Showing the actual opening that the 120mm case was ejected from. In this case the armoured door is missing and the large framework above the turret is carried for targets, as this is a second life for this vehicle after being withdrawn from service.

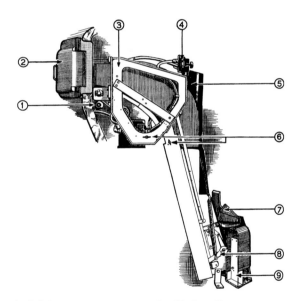

1. Main motor
2. Door
3. Upper frame
4. Isolating switch
5. Stop plate
6. Chain adjusters
7. Cartridge case aligner
8. Control arm
9. Starter switch casing

A drawing from the Conqueror gunnery manual showing all the components of the Mollins ejector gear and naming all the main parts. This shows how complex a system it was. Courtesy of MoD.

would be ejected from the gun and land onto a carrier on the turret floor. This in turn closed a microswitch which activated a series of chain drives, which carried the case up a chute to the ejection door which would open automatically. The system then would reset itself ready for the next round, the whole cycle taking about 5 seconds.

The idea in concept was admirable, but in practice it was very rare for it to work. The design for this equipment was given to the firm who manufactured 90 per cent of the world's cigarette and similar types of coin-operated machines. If you have ever lost money in one of those dispensers you may feel some sympathy for the poor loader when the equipment broke down. When this happened there were two ways of clearing the turret – one was for the loader to throw the hot cases out of the turret, no mean feat as the cases weighed 25lb (11kg) even when empty; he would also have to put on gloves as the case would still be hot, all the while trying to keep up a high rate of loading. The alternative to this was for the commander to use the emergency winding handle provided for just such an occasion, then, on the case reaching a certain position, he would pull a rope, the ejection door in the turret would open and out the case would fall. This was all right if it was only for one case, but during a gunnery camp the commander had more to

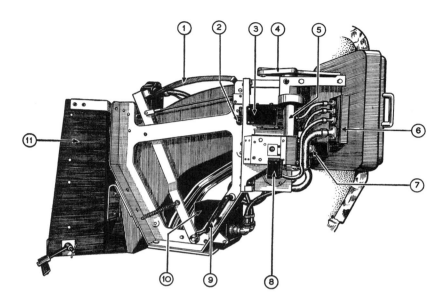

1. Hand ejector
2. Pull-roe knob
3. Timing switch
4. Door linkage
5. Door operating shaft
6. Junction box
7. Down interlock switch
8. Hand interlock switch
9. Handle
10. Control box
11. Stop plate

A more detailed drawing from the gunnery manual showing the top mechanism of the ejector gear. Courtesy of MoD.

Showing the case ejector gear working. Note the case in mid-air, also the three cases on the floor. The empty cases lined up behind the vehicle will be lined up in groups of five or ten to enable them to be accounted for easily. Note the smoke forming at the muzzle. This is a good example of the fume being cleared from the barrel by the fume extractor, the large round object visible halfway up the barrel.

	Centurion 3	FV201	FV221	FV214
General				
Weight (lb)	110,000	122,000	134,400	134,400
Length (in)	297	306	306	306
Width (in)	132 $\frac{3}{4}$	156	156	156
Turret ring (in)	74	74–79	80	80
Ground pressure	12.8	9.84	11	11
Crew	4	5	4	4
Performance				
HP/ton	13	15.6	14.5	14.5
Speed mph	21.5	19	17	21.3
Radius (miles)	84	110	100	100
Armour (in)				
Hull				
Glacis upper	3 at 57°	3 at 60°	5 at 60°	5 at 60°
Glacis lower	3 at 45°	3 at 45°	5 at 60°	5 at 60°
Rear	1at 60°–90°	1 at 80°	1 at 90°	1 at 90°
Sides	1 at 11°	2 at 60°	2 at 90°	2 at 90°
Bottom	$\frac{2}{3}$	$\frac{3}{4}$	$\frac{3}{4}$	$\frac{3}{4}$
Turret				
Front	6	6	8	8
Side	3 at 15°	3 at 15°	3	3
Gun shield	none	none	none	none
Weapons ammo fire control				
Main armament	20pdr	20pdr	20pdr	120mm
No. of rounds	65	75	75	35
Stabilizer	yes	yes	yes	yes*
Range finder	no	yes	no	yes
Auto loader	no	no	no	no
Engine				
Type	Meteor IV	Meteor PI	Meteor II	Meteor II
Bhp	640/2850	800/2000	860/2800	860/2800

*While Conqueror did not have full stabilization fitted, this was a form of it and it allowed the gun to move within set limits if the vehicle moved above 1.5mph.

worry about than trying to eject empty cases. The emergency hand-winding system was also very tiring and time-consuming. The first case could probably be wound out in about 30 seconds, but by the time the commander had reached number five it would probably take more like several minutes.

One high spot of the Mollins ejector gear system was that no matter how many times visiting officers were warned to be careful of empty cases flying through the air, they would always seem to stand just by the ejection hatch. Luckily no serious accidents have been recorded, but much entertainment was provided to the watching crews.

The cause of the majority of the systems' failures was well known but to remove it completely would have meant several design changes which would have probably delayed the introduction of the vehicle even further, a situation that the General Staff were not prepared to accept. We shall, however, hear more about the Mollins ejector gear later.

There were many more problems that befell the production line of Conqueror. Some were simple and easily rectified, whilst others were more complicated and were never completely resolved; yet others were due to industrial action. In spite of this, the British Army eventually got its 60-ton, long-range sniper into service.

On the preceding page is a chart produced by DRAC in response to a question from the Director of Finance. Some of the figures are dubious, such as turret protection given to FV221; it should be the same as for Centurion III as both carried the same turret. Nevertheless, it does give us an idea as to how things were presented during the battle for Conqueror.

3 Trials and Service

CONQUEROR ARRIVES IN SECRECY

The introduction at last of Conqueror to the regiments of the RAC was almost as shambolic an affair as its development and production had been. It is almost as though the regiments had absolutely no idea of its arrival, to quote one REME Staff Sergeant at the time, 'Conqueror seemed to sneak into the unit over the weekend. On Friday we had locked up our vehicle hangars with our Centurions inside and on Monday when the doors were opened there were these three great big beasts.' This type of remark is very common and much the same for most units, the general impression being that the regiments were poorly prepared for Conquerors' arrival, and REME, through no fault of their own, were even worse off.

Such remarks are probably not far from the truth, as for reasons of security Conqueror was in fact delivered to its units under a great shroud of secrecy. At the time of its introduction the Cold War was reaching its most confrontational period, with the Soviet Union and the Western powers desperate to discover all that they could about each other's military hardware. The following journey described by Sergeant (now Captain) B. D. Patrick of the Intelligence Corps is very typical.

Sgt Patrick recalls that sometime in 1955 he was serving with 93 field security section based at Lüneburg. They were informed that a convoy of 'special equipment' was to be kept free from prying eyes both whilst static and on the move through Germany. This convoy turned out to consist of four Antars each with a shrouded Conqueror on board. Two West German police cars, two Royal Military Police vehicles, RASC motorcycle outriders, a spare Antar tractor unit, one Scammel recovery vehicle, one 3-ton truck with REME fitters, and one Volkswagen with the field security NCOs accompanied the convoy. Trying to keep that little group a secret must have been a rather daunting task. The convoy met up for the first time on the docks at Hamburg where the Conquerors had been offloaded and guarded by a full company of Cameronians who were stationed nearby.

This first convoy was destined for Hohne and in all the journey took 12½ hours. To anyone who knows that route that is an awfully long time, and the reason was that the combined height of Conqueror on top of the Antar trailer created a formidable structure. That meant that every time the convoy arrived at a bridge which went over the autobahn the tanks had to be unloaded, and transporter and tank driven under the bridge and then reloaded. Remember as well that there were three tanks in the convoy and the timescale begins to make sense. At every unloading the security team had to ensure that the heavily sheeted turrets were not compromised in any way.

Once the convoy had left the autobahn, its troubles were not over by a long way as the road from the autobahn to Hohne garrison had to cross a small stream, and as luck would have it the stream doubled back on itself three times. The bridges that crossed the stream were not strong enough to take the convoy's weight so the unloading process started all over again. There was not much of an alternative, as the all-up weight of Antar and Conqueror was in the region of 120 tons (121,920kg).

During the movement of the second convoy the following night, at one of the bridge crossing points near Hohne the security section apprehended a German civilian taking photographs from the cover of nearby shrubbery. He was duly arrested and handed over to the German civil police for questioning, and later charged with the crime of illegally photographing military equipment.

We can see now that our REME S/Sgt was nearly correct when he said that the Conqueror*s* appeared to have sneaked into the hangars over the weekend, or as well as 60 tons of large, noisy fighting vehicle can sneak any where.

Having at long last managed to get their hands on the vehicles the 4/7th Royal Dragoon Guards at Fallingbostel soon found a problem which it seems that no-one had considered. They were housed in ex-German Army barracks and whilst the hangars might have been suitable for the vehicles from World War II, Conqueror, with its great overhang of barrel, would not fit in. The solution was novel if not ideal – the carpenters cut holes in the doors, the tanks were driven in and the gun elevated and traversed so that it was in line with the cut-out and then the doors were secured. The view of all the Conqueror's barrels poking out of the holes in the doors must have been reminiscent of the old Cavalry days with the horses looking from the stable door.

One of the more unusual pictures of Conqueror showing the measures that the 4th/7th Royal Dragoon Guards were forced to adopt to close the doors on their Conquerors in their ex-German Army hangars at Fallingbostel, West Germany. Courtesy of Soldier *magazine.*

TROOP TRIALS BEGIN

However, Conqueror had at last arrived and the first twenty vehicles were deployed on troop trials. Up to this point, the only information on handling such a large vehicle had come from the trials conducted using Caernarvon. While this had given up valuable information it did not provide the full picture, as Caernarvon possessed only the Centurion III turret. It also had shock absorbers on front and rear wheel stations. However, if we look at some of the surviving report material we find that overall Caernarvon had proved its worth. The two vehicles that were sent to the MELF with the 14/20th Hussars

based in Tripoli achieved a mileage of 2,087 (3,360 km) for 07 BA 74 and 2,062 (3,320km) for 07 BA 75. 07 BA 74 was unserviceable for some time due to lack of spares, and was occasionally cannibalized to keep the other vehicles roadworthy. The report stressed that it was the FV221 that was being reported on and not the FV214. This might seem obvious, but some people in the War Office were still opposed to Conqueror and would have gladly taken the reports out of context.

It was decided that it would be totally impracticable to run the trial based in camp, so the whole lot moved 70 miles out into the desert, which also meant that no

Showing the comparative width of Conqueror and Centurion. The bulk and length of Conqueror can clearly be seen in this shot. Courtesy M. Hiscock.

main REME workshop would be available for major repairs. In the end, all repairs were done in the desert, thus providing the fitters with valuable experience in the handling and fault-finding of such a large vehicle. It was stated that the high mileage achieved during these trials was due to the fact that the troops were based in the desert and not in camp. The report goes on to list various faults, but overall it was felt that the vehicle was capable of excellent performance. This report still exists today and a letter written concerning the preliminary report was addressed to Capt. McClure of the 14/20th. It was written by a man signing himself Reg (TOM) and the tone of the letter suggests that he may well have been a friend of Capt. McClure as the good Captain signs himself as 'Ubendum'! The tone of the letter is one of pleasure and possibly surprise 'that after 2,000 miles the vehicle is still capable of this sort of performance without falling to bits!' On a final note, the CinC Far East Forces commended the regimental personnel on a job well done.

P2, showing that the final form for Conqueror is nearly there. Of interest are the weights bolted on to the turret top and sides and glacis plate. This is a common practice during the prototype stage and is used to add weight to simulate the all-up weight of the production vehicle. Courtesy of Tank Museum.

07 BA 75, one of the Caernarvons pictured during the desert trials as part of the MELF. The shock absorbers fitted to Caernarvon can be clearly seen on the front and rear suspension units. Although this is the desert note how the crew are dressed warmly. Tank Museum.

The other vehicles were subjected to various trials, such as trying to make the vehicle shed its track (it could not), time taken to replenish ammunition from various locations within the vehicle and speed tests with a new vehicle and at various mileages thereafter.

To go into the testing of the FV221 would take a book in itself and would not provide the most interesting of reads, it is safe to say that with the Caernarvon trials over, all the interested parties now had some idea of what was to come. Those who had taken part in the trials and would later receive Conqueror could only hope that the bad points they had raised would be rectified.

After arriving in great secrecy, now was the time to find out what the problems were going to be with the revolutionary layout of the turret and the vehicle in the hands of the actual user and not a trials team,

An unusual view of Caernarvon during the desert trials. This illustrates rather nicely how a track-laying vehicle's track enables it to cross gaps. Tank Museum.

Prototype vehicle on trials at FVRDE Chertsey fitted with the Windsor turret. As can be seen, the vehicle has become well and truly bogged in the muddy ground. To retrieve this vehicle it was eventually necessary to cut off both tracks. Courtesy DRA Chertsey Crown copyrights.

who sometimes by their dedication tend to make things work that perhaps might not under operational circumstances.

The twenty trials vehicles plus one late arrival that had been equipped with disc brakes (40 BA 79) were issued to various regiments, although not all received the normal allocation of nine vehicles. The trials programme was very full and comprehensive and it achieved its aim of highlighting the vehicle's good and bad points. However, the 4th/7th Royal Dragoon Guards also felt that the trials programme lacked that certain something, and so managed to create a test that had not been set up in the programme. This involved running two vehicles into each other, causing so much damage to one, 40

BA 96, that it took no further part in the trials and was slowly cannibalized as a ready source of spares, until it was returned to the UK for a full rebuild. This, it must be noted, was not intentional and was a pure accident, as was the occasion when A Squadron 4th/7th Royal Dragoon Guards did it again some twenty-five years later with two Chieftains, and nose to nose as well.

The troop trials vehicles were a mix of Mk Is and IIs and this caused further problems with the reporting of faults as the two vehicles had a certain number of differences. In July 1955 there was a concentration of Conquerors on Hohne ranges, which must have been impressive. All twenty BAOR vehicles were there and all managed to fire.

Due mainly to the priority given to the repair of Conqueror, all vehicles remained on the road for the greater part of the summer, by which time all the vehicles had completed excessive mileage, with one vehicle recording over 1,000 miles (1,609km). In addition, all tanks had fired at least ten main armament rounds.

The reporting procedure throughout the trial worked very well (no mean feat on its own), and most of the information required was obtained. However, any further trials were forced to await delivery of the new fuel tanks to replace the originals which had been constructed to a lower standard than required. The enforced waiting period had the benefit of allowing the information so far gleaned to be assimilated.

REPORTING BACK

By November 1955, the technical branch of the Rhine Army had prepared a draft report on the outcome of the trials, and as expected it produced a lot of problems, although this is not an unusual occurrence for a new vehicle undergoing trials. Some of the problems that were found included a worryingly low chance of a hit with HESH, fuel tanks leaking (still), and the lack of provision for hand traverse of the FCT. Vehicles fitted with a straight-through exhaust system, mostly the Mk IIs,

Rebuilt Caernarvon during firing trials at the RAC Gunnery School at Lulworth in Dorset. The figure seated on top of the turret is the gunnery instructor and not a member of the crew.

were also found to be noisy. Opinion was unanimously negative regarding the fitting of only one driver's periscope to the Mk IIs as it was felt that the field of view from the single periscope was totally inadequate when compared to the three periscopes fitted to the Mk I vehicles.

Some proposals that were put forward, although conceived with the best intentions, were never feasible. One such idea was that due to the complexity of the vehicle the only people who should be allowed to command it should be at least subalterns or SNCOs, all of whom for the foreseeable future should have been trained at the Gunnery school at Lulworth. This idea was not totally accepted and although officers and SNCOs did command it, this was to fulfil the normal

crewing arrangements and not as a result of this recommendation. Also, each regiment had different ideas about how the vehicle was to be used within the squadrons, combined with the fact that units could not afford to lose officers and senior NCOs on long courses in the UK. The report also managed to halt some outlandish ideas that had been suggested by desk-bound tank commanders in London, such as the idea noted earlier of copying the American system with two crews per vehicle, one to man it and the other to take over when the vehicle came into a hide at night. This second crew would carry out all replenishment and maintenance required. This might have looked good on paper but to quote from the report 'although the task of replenishing and maintaining Conqueror in the field

This shows P5 having its engine removed by a Bedford repair vehicle. This was to prove whether the Bedford would be up to carrying out this role in the field. Courtesy DERA Chertsey Crown Copyright.

P5 07 BA 68 with what looks like a successful lift of the engine and the Bedford seems to have stayed upright all right. DERA Chertsey Crown Copyright.

40 BA 98 with a very smart crew from the 4/7 RDG. This was one of the trials vehicles and later was in collision with 40 BA 96. Courtesy Soldier *Magazine.*

is an arduous task, experience to date suggests that any form of maintenance crew would be a luxury.' The other problem would have been in finding enough trained crew who would be spare to carry out that function.

Perhaps the one item of the report that was to be repeated again and again was the breakdown of the Mollins ejection system, coupled with the amount of time that it took to use the emergency system, with periods of up to five minutes being quoted. The remark that it was quicker to throw the empty case out of the loader's hatch, whilst just about acceptable for training, would not be of any use in an operational situation. There would also be the problem of the loader having to put on gloves to handle the hot case, then remove them to carry on loading, as gloves are forbidden to be worn by loaders.

The report runs to many pages and deals with just about every aspect of the tank. Many of the suggestions were very minor, whilst others should have constituted a major rethink of the tank's design. This did happen in some cases, but sadly a large amount was ignored. This attitude was to play a large part in the operational use of Conqueror throughout its short life. It may be that pressure was brought to bear on bypassing a lot of the trial comments, for as we have seen it was not going to

Unloading Conquerors at Soltau training area in Germany. Note the very steep angle that is adopted during loading/unloading. The sheet on the turret is usually fitted to protect the vehicle and the crew kit from the elements during transit.

To all who have served on tanks in Germany on Soltau, this will be a familiar scene. It gives an idea of the type of conditions that a tank must work in. The vehicle right at the rear is a Centurion ARV.

The same two Conquerors, showing how much up and down movement is involved in cross-country work.

Three crew members of a 4/7 RDG Conqueror at Fallingbostel, West Germany. Note the use of camouflage net around the turret in an attempt to break up the very distinctive outline.

A 4/7 RDG Conqueror on the Soltau training area. Note again the use of netting around the rear of the turret and over the mantlet.

be acceptable for the FV214 not to be accepted for service.

Conqueror's performance and tactical handling were found to be far better than a lot of people had predicted. On road marches it was able to keep up with Centurion and on a good, firm straight road it actually could have the edge on Centurion in speed by about 1.5mph. However, if the route were based on narrow roads with lots of bends and villages then it would start to lag behind. Apart from the weight restrictions on bridges and culverts Conqueror could accompany Centurion on any road march. One observation in the trial report, which really seems rather obvious, is that Conqueror seemed to cause more damage to the roads than Centurion – hardly surprising, considering Centurion's 56 tons and 24in tracks against Conqueror's 65 tons and 31in tracks!

Over rough ground, it was found that Conqueror was less likely to become bogged than Centurion, but Centurion was faster over rough ground than Conqueror, unless Conqueror was driven really hard. It was found that the choice of hides and harbour locations was not affected by the deployment of Conqueror, although most locations that had been used were mainly based on a peacetime setting.

The crew positions were reported on in some detail, and we shall look at just some of the salient points here. The concept of the commander's sights and rangefinding equipment was good and it was felt that the eyepieces were placed in the most convenient location for use by the commander. All instruments were considered to be of a high optical standard, except the rangefinder (as we have already seen). Most commanders stated that their preferred method of using the FCT was to use the no. 6 sight (the central periscope) and scan traversing the FCT. The need for hand traverse as stated in the report was felt to be vital for four main reasons: the commander must be able to take the FCT to the 12 o'clock position in the event of power failure; The commander must be able to traverse to reach the spare boxes of .30 ammo for his machine gun; escape facilities would be helped if hand traverse were incorporated into the system; and it would be of major use in routine servicing and maintenance.

The Browning machine gun on the FCT proved to be a useful and popular weapon, and great importance was attached to it, as it was the only offensive weapon that could be fired on the move. However, once the vehicle entered general service, some doubts were expressed about its usefulness. The main complaint, as already noted, was the Mollins ejector gear and this was never satisfactorily sorted out. The design and layout of the FCT was good and the recommendation to select commanders in particular was not adhered to, as a man capable of using the facilities provided could fight the tank effectively.

The gunner's station was in general a good one provided that the selected gunner was not the tall, broad type, otherwise he might find it a bit of a tight fit. No obvious way could be seen to increase the space available for the gunner, and it was felt that the position was satisfactory for it did not cause the gunner undue fatigue or confusion and the facilities provided would enable him to carry out his task in battle.

The major faults with the gunner's station concerned the position of the powered elevation controller. This fouled the gunner's right knee, and the hand elevation wheel was located so that in use the gunner would catch his knuckles on it, and on some vehicles the wheel itself fouled the gunner's shield. This was solved later by fitting a handle instead of a wheel, and the whole system was inconsistent and prone to failure. A traverse indicator was considered essential, and in fact steps

had already been taken to produce one. The gunner could scan using his x1 sight for long periods of time, whether the tank was static or moving so long as the gun was stabilized, without suffering from confusion or fatigue.

The crew position that provoked a long series of discussions was surprisingly that of the loader, for the design had not provided the loader with his own periscope, something which had almost become traditional in British AFV design. In the end, it was decided that it would have to be accepted, but that the situation was 'most undesirable'. Nothing could be done to rectify this fault on the turret that was then available, although serious consideration was given to reintroducing the loader's periscope. The extra periscope is useful, for until the loader is tied down with loading drills, he can provide an extra pair of eyes for scanning the ground in front.

It was felt that bearing in mind the size of the ammunition the stowage was satisfactory, although one worry concerning ammunition was the fact that both the HESH and APDS cases looked exactly the same. In the heat of action or live firing there was nothing to prevent the loader putting a HESH projectile in the chamber, followed by a APDS charge, which whilst not endangering the vehicle would be particularly impressive to any onlooker

Showing the FCT with the .30 Browning and its ammunition box, the bracket in the background is used to hold the commander's hatch in either the fully open position or in the umbrella position. In the foreground can be seen the armoured cover for the left-hand head of the rangefinder.

expecting to see the slow flight of a HESH round, but which would exit the barrel a lot faster. Until a means to differentiate them was found, the only answer lay in training. In the Chieftain the same problem could have occurred, except that the charges were made two different lengths; in addition, the HESH charge for Chieftain was only half the diameter.

Access to the radios was good and the loader could reach all auxiliary controls that he might require, and the removal of toxic fumes from the co-axial gun was very good. It was in the area of fitness that the loader tended to suffer – with no vision device available for use when the vehicle was closed down and moving with the stabilizer on, the loaders tended to complain of feeling confused, travel sick and discouraged. It was felt, therefore, that the loader would need to be selected on his physical strength, and that this high state of physical fitness would need to be maintained. He

would also have to be very familiar with the vehicle.

The cause of this problem was the size and weight of the ammunition rather than the design of the vehicle, for within these constraints the loader's station was satisfactory. A fully instrumented trial to assess the amount of loader fatigue was therefore requested, and RAC Gunnery School at Lulworth conducted this trial.

The driver's station was the least controversial of the four, as almost of the problems had already been identified from the user trials involving Caernarvon. The main criticism regarding the closed-down position was that there was a lack of space for the driver to rest his left foot clear of the clutch. In the opened-up position drivers were coming to terms with the new style of hatch; prior to the introduction of the lift-and-swing design drivers' hatches were usually in two parts and lifted up to open. The incidence of drivers not securing

Showing how the 120mm ammunition was stored in the turret, with the projectiles above the turret ring but with the brass propellant case safely stored below turret ring level. Note the marking on the HESH round head, showing that it is an experimental round.

Compare this picture with that of the experimental round – this is an in-service HESH round. The copper ring at the base of the round when fired will be cut into by the rifling in the barrel, thus imparting spin to the projectile.

120mm APDS. What is seen here is the outer casing or sabot that will fly off when the round leaves the gun, as the armour penetrating core needs to be much smaller in diameter than 120mm to achieve high muzzle velocity. It is supported by the sabot whilst in the gun during firing. The white nylon bands that can be seen top and bottom are cut by the rifling and this allows the sabot to fall away on leaving the muzzle.

the hatch correctly soon led to some sore faces, but once the mistake had been made it never happened again.

Time had also been taken to study how long it would take to remove a casualty from each crew station, both conscious and unconscious. The results are as shown opposite. These figures are not too bad considering the extent to which crew members were isolated from each other in the vehicle, and so in that sense the facilities were considered as good. The salient point here is that the times were in ideal conditions, with no-one trying

Crew Member	Conscious	Unconscious
Commander	10–30 secs	20–60 secs
Gunner	10–30 secs	20–60 secs
Driver	10–30 secs	10–30 secs
Gunner	20–60 secs	up to 2 mins

to kill the crew whilst the evacuation of the injured crew member was being carried out.

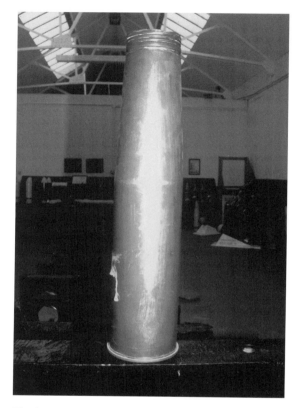

The brass propellant case, which was common to both HESH and APDS. In the background can be seen Chieftain 120mm HESH smoke and HESH practice.

TAKING DELIVERY

With the trials over, the vehicle now was issued to the regiments, which should have been ready to receive them and able to crew them as by now the tanks were a familiar sight, at least in BAOR. However, this did not prove to be the case. The experience of 3rd Royal Tank Regiment appeared to be common. Regimental Gunnery Sergeant Alan Simcock (now retired WO2 Simcock BEM) has stated that when 3RTR received their first tanks in 1957 the regiment was poorly prepared for their arrival, and he himself had only been shown briefly a pre-production vehicle at Lulworth in 1955. However, as luck would have it one of the

regiment's sergeants had just completed his long gunnery course, during which he had had a short familiarization course on Conqueror which enabled conversion courses to be set up. It is about at this point that a very telling statement from ex-RQMS Dennis Redfearn of the 4/7RDG must be noted: ignorance was the Conqueror's biggest enemy. Unfortunately, this ignorance was always prevalent at the command level of the regiments, with commanding officers sometimes being the worst offenders.

This situation seems to have been prevalent throughout the Royal Armoured Corps and not just within one regiment. It was felt that the Conqueror was simply a tank, therefore if a soldier was a Centurion crewman there was no reason why he could not work as well on Conqueror. Such a blinkered view was very hard to overcome. Indeed, it still exists today. My own example is that on the return of my regiment to BAOR in the early seventies we were issued with the Stalwart high-mobility vehicle. Due to the fact that it was a novelty compared to the standard Bedford RL 3-ton truck, it was used as a general runaround, although the qualified drivers tried to explain that Stalwart was meant to be used cross-country, and so using it like this was no good for it. However, they were ignored with the result that the vehicle suffered many problems that could have been avoided. In later years this was stopped and the vehicle was taken by rail to exercise areas to prevent damage.

The other main problem for Conqueror was the allocation of vehicles within the regiment, which had originally been intended to be nine per regiment. This in itself was an unusual figure as it was not enough to equip each tank troop with one Conqueror, which is how it had been originally envisaged to be used, with the Centurions moving in their normal tactical formation and the Conqueror sat one tactical bound behind in an overwatch position ready to take on the JS3 should it appear. 3 RTR used this method and issued one vehicle to each nominated troop. Whilst 4/7DG had six tanks deployed into two troops – one in A Sqn with the others going to C Sqn – these troops were crewed as per a normal tank troop, i.e. officer sergeant and corporal. This formation did change later to one Conqueror per troop. QRIH had one Centurion and two Conquerors each troop. 1RTR had a Conqueror troop per squadron but this was later changed to one Conqueror per tank troop. Other suggestions put forward included the idea from the 9th Lancers in Detmold that the vehicles should be grouped together and formed into a Heavy Squadron. Whatever method was chosen, Conqueror had at last arrived and it was now time for the troops to get used to it and prepare for the training cycle with their new vehicle. It was also a chance to find out if all the horror stories that had filtered back were true or not.

Most regiments had by now started to run their own internal courses while still trying to overcome the 'one tank is very much the same as another syndrome'. One problem that very soon became apparent in the training of the loaders was that of physique. It soon became obvious that some crewmen who were earmarked as loaders would be incapable of lifting the large separated case ammunition which weighed some 21lb (9.5kg) for a APDS projectile and 35lb (16kg) for HESH, with the case weighing in at 43lb (20kg). This resulted in some crew changes as well as giving the physical

training instructors something to do as strength-building exercises were used to help the loaders. By now, a loader trainer had been issued and this helped tremendously, although requests for fired cartridge cases to be supplied as a training aid and to help set up the Mollins gear seemed to fall on deaf ears. Experienced gunners had no problem converting to the new system, but the less experienced found it all rather daunting.

CONQUEROR IN ACTION

Regardless of all the problems that seemed to present themselves, crews were trained and at last it was time to put all the training to good use as Conqueror started to take part in the normal exercise periods that filled a regiment's year. The reaction of the crews to the vehicle in its natural environment was mixed. Cpl (later WO1) Willie Greig of the 4/7DG tells us:

During my time with Conqueror I was first of all a L/Cpl driver and then Cpl Commander and I liked the vehicle a lot. Of course, there were problems but most of them you could overcome if you worked at them. The FCT had its good and

Showing the size of 120mm ammunition compared to 20-pounder, with HESH front left, APDS right and 120mm cases in the rear with the 20-pounder ammunition centre. The round objects in the background are the packing and transit case for the ammunition.

bad points; it was the first time that the troops had an accurate method of finding the range to a target. Prior to this, if you wanted to engage a tank with APDS you could either guess the range or hope your luck was in, or employ a method known as HESH ranging where the commander estimated the range to the target and then fired a HESH round. The subsequent APDS round would then be fired taking into account information taken from observing the fall of shot. Both methods really lent themselves more to the days of 1944 than to a modern vehicle. The major disadvantage with this method was that once you had fired your position was given away, and you risked being engaged yourself.

The big problem with the FCT was that for the first time in the RAC the commander was totally isolated from the remainder of his turret crew, so you had to hope that you had a first-class crew

otherwise you could have big problems. It also meant that you could not deliver the traditional kick into the gunner's back to remind him that he had got it badly wrong.

There were times when I was commanding my Chieftain that the power traverse failed which meant that we had to travel with the gun in the crutch. This forced the commander to spend all his time kneeling on the commander's seat, a position to be avoided if at all possible for any length of time. It was at times like this that I must admit to a yearning for the FCT of Conqueror.

One interesting trial carried out at this time gave much food for thought and a serious review of tactics. 3RTR as part of 4 Div were tasked to play the friendly forces to defend the high ground whilst the remainder of the brigade attacked in the manner of a Soviet mass formation. When the 'enemy'

Conqueror at high speed. The commander has got the FCT reversed. Possibly the powered gun kit has broken down and they have had to travel with the gun in the travelling crutch.

Camouflaged and muddy, the Conqueror of the Queen's Own Hussars on Salisbury Plain. Courtesy J. Chappell.

Conqueror crews of Queen's Own Hussars getting ready for exercise on Salisbury Plain. Note also the Centurion alongside. Courtesy J. Chappell.

The Conqueror crewman seems to have a very haughty view of his compatriot in the Centurion next to him. Notice how the Centurion crew have used camouflage net to cover the barrel of their gun. Courtesy of J. Chappell.

This crew seems to be taking a break, with one of them risking trouble by smoking on an armoured vehicle!

broke cover the Centurions only picked them up at about 300m range, and then only for a brief time. It was, as the Americans would say, 'a turkey shoot'. The Conqueror crews managed to engage about two targets before they were overrun, and although the conditions were a bit artificial it did make people stop and think.

The crews were finding out just what they could do with the vehicle and most were delighted to find that it could in fact get to places that a Centurion could not. Also Conqueror had the slight edge in speed and so quite often was employed as lead vehicle for road marches, a position that it should not have been filling. Most people can remember the effect of a troop of Conquerors moving down a metalled road. The noise was quite fearsome. As G.T. Smith of 1RTR recalls, 'when Conqueror was up and running it really was an awesome beast. The fuel-injected engine really had a powerful sound to it and the sheer size and appearance of it made it look formidable.' Others were not so lavish in their praise, however. As Tpr Ron Kerr 4/7DG stated 'I can't really think of one good thing to say about it. If you actually made it to the exercise area then the best that you could hope for was maybe about 20 miles and then a major breakdown, leaving you there till the end of the exercise.' To be fair, some of the problems were self-inflicted by the 'you are a Centurion man so you will be OK on Conqueror syndrome'. To quote G.T. Smith again, 'The crews that I can remember liked it for the masses of space and like all squaddies they loved the engine noise produced by the straight-through exhaust system. I seem to remember not having to change as many road wheels as when I worked on Centurion, but at the end of the day I had no regrets about it being withdrawn.'

One feature that was of great annoyance to the crews was the decision not to give Conqueror as good a stabilization system as Centurion, as it had been decided that the requirement for engaging targets on the move would not apply to Conqueror as it was to be a support tank. There was a stabilizer fitted, but at speeds of over 1.5mph a mercury sensing switch took over and kept the gun within set limits with the gunner having very little control over it. This also precluded any ideas of firing on the move, as the loader would have been very hard pressed to keep up, considering the size of the brass cases. The other problem caused by this was the delay in the equipment returning control to the gunner once the vehicle had come to a halt. Many are the Centurion crewmen who said that whilst they may not have seen Conqueror moving from one fire position to another, all you had to do was sit and wait. Very soon you would see a 120mm barrel waving aimlessly in the air for those vital few seconds until the gunner regained control.

This system also caused some people to see another problem, in that with the gunner not having full control of the gun on the move it was potentially fatal for the loader to try to do anything about any stoppages on the .30 Browning machine gun whilst on the move. This, however, was not perceived as a major problem as Gunnery School teaching did not allow the loader to attempt to clear stoppages on the co-axial machine gun whilst on the move. This was purely for peacetime safety regulations, and would no doubt be changed for combat situations

Conqueror's performance on the range was again a very mixed showing, although after seeing the 120mm gun fired for the first time most Centurion crews were of the opinion that they felt a lot better knowing that Conqueror was in the overwatch position ready to take out the JS3. It certainly would have removed JS3 from the battlefield in no uncertain terms, as Conqueror, with at least a 1,000m advantage, could off pick the JS3 before it got within range. Surprisingly, a lot of the figures relating to Conqueror's 120mm gun are still classified, but the few figures available show that if nothing else was right at least the gun would do its job. 3RTR were lucky in that during one of their first range periods they were presented with a virgin hard target in the form of a 25-pounder Sexton SP, and the chance was taken to show just what HESH could do to an armoured vehicle. One round of HESH was fired at a range of 1,000m and a first-round hit obtained. Once the range was cleared everyone took a trip down range to view the end result, where they were greeted by a most heartening sight. Just as the gunnery book had told them, a large scab had come away from the armour, the inside had been devastated and certainly no crew would have survived.

Other people remember the ranges for other reasons. Lt (now Brigadier, retd) Gilruth 4/7DG recalls spending the day firing HESH at hard targets. In the evening when firing was over, the REME fitters would go down range and flame cut-out any part of the target that had been hit by HESH and remove it, also removing any portions of the scabs that remained. This was due to the fact even in 1958 the results of a HESH strike were still classified.

The single most repetitive complaint as regards firing periods was that concerning the Mollins gear, as already mentioned. No real attempt to rectify the problem was ever made, even though plenty of suggestions had been put forward, so the result was a system that was next to useless.

The time that was wasted by commanders having to wind up the empty case manually and work the ejection door by hand could easily be five minutes. Trying to throw the cases out of the loader's hatch resulted in several loaders receiving burns to their faces when they lost control of the case, which

although empty was still heavy and awkward to handle. The Mollins system when it was inoperative killed dead the effectiveness of having a 120mm-gunned vehicle as it reduced the rate of fire so much. However, when all the systems were working 100 per cent, then it was a truly awesome sight to see the Conqueror firing. If the need had arisen to use the tank in anger then its capability to engage targets out to 2,500m and its ability to penetrate the armour of JS3 at 1,000m with APDS and at all ranges with HESH would have been a great comfort. In addition, the glacis plate would defeat the 122mm gun of the JS3.

Transportation of the Conqueror also posed problems, although in the end not as bad as had been predicted. Like all tracked vehicles, Conqueror could only travel a certain amount of miles on its own tracks. This is known as track mileage and still affects vehicles today. The obvious solution is to move the vehicles around by means of railways or tank transporters. The big worry was that at 65 tons Conqueror's weight was more than the current British tank transporters could manage. However, at about the same time that Conqueror was coming into service so was the Thornycroft Antar, which proved more than capable of taking the weight. The German railway

All that remains of 41 BA 23 after years on Castlemartin ranges in Wales. It has been attacked by HESH and APDS, thus ending its days still giving service to its country.

41 BA 23, again showing the neat round holes in the turret caused by APDS. This also shows to good effect the wall thickness of the hull side armour.

system could also successfully manage Conqueror due to the rather more generous loading dimensions used as compared to British railways.

However, loading onto rail flats was not that easy and it was always a manoeuvre that seemed to take place at about 3am on a cold and wet morning and anyone with memories of loading Centurion or Chieftain who thought that they had problems should have tried loading Conqueror. The main person in charge was always a German railway worker, who used to take measurements at each

corner of the track overhang. Inevitably, they would be greater on one side than the other, which meant trying to move a 65-ton tank with all the grace and skill of a ballet dancer. Usually the only solution was to reverse off and try to line up again. This precise lining up was very important because even allowing for the large loading gauge allowed, a train with Conqueror on board only had about 3in of space either side of bridges and tunnels, and when the train passed through a station the tracks were overhanging the platform.

Nicely turned out Conqueror belonging to the 5th Inniskilling Dragoon Guards on Hohne ranges, West Germany in 1959. The flag flying from the FCT would have been a red one to show that the tank was at action and the gun was loaded, when clear a green flag would be flown.

The Conqueror of 13/18 Hussars loading onto Antar tank transporters at Sennelager, West Germany. From this picture it can be seen how blind the driver is on a manoeuvre like this.

Success – all loaded up and ready to go. The vehicle driver would travel with the transporter crew who would either be from the RASC or from an organization known as MSO. This was made up of displaced persons who worked for the British forces and gave many years of loyal service to the British crown. The job was sometimes in the same family for several generations.

A final check before the move out. In this shot, it is apparent just how wide Conqueror is by the overhang of the tracks on the transporter.

Other problems were a distinct lack of spares for the vehicle compared to the back-up that Centurion enjoyed. Also, anyone who has never tried to camouflage something as large as Conqueror has no idea what they have missed, as it was a very difficult vehicle to try to hide or cover with a camouflage net. There were other problems that made trying to conceal a Conqueror very difficult, such as the long barrel of the main armament, and the high profile created by the FCT and its machine gun. There were also the dark shadows cast by the turret bustle, the very distinctive bazooka plates and the shadows cast by them, and the very boxy square shape to the rear end of the vehicle. Three main noises enabled Conqueror to be identified from quite a long distance: the roar from the straight-through exhaust;

the need to run the main engine every twenty minutes or so to help cool the aux-generator (provision of electric fan drives cured this problem later); and finally the very distinctive fan whine of a vehicle on the move.

On the ranges, some outstanding problems still needed attention. The target acquisition was faster than Centurion's, but the time taken to fire the first round could be up to two minutes in some cases. This was far too long, and so the rate of fire was not as high as had been hoped for. The Mk I rangefinder was proving to be of no real use and it was felt that the information given by this instrument was no better than that obtained using the Mk I eyeball. The solution to this was that in the next summer (1958) it was hoped to be able to fit the Mk II rangefinder

41 BA 71 sporting a rather different type of camouflage. This is chicken wire with copper filings bonded to it and in time they will go green because of verdigis and it was hoped would act as a camouflage – yet another idea that did not quite make it.

and also to start trials with the fitting of a .50 spotting rifle to the vehicle. It was suggested that pending the outcome of those trials it might well be prudent to introduce the .50 spotting rifle anyway. In the end, it never happened and the spotting rifle appeared first on Centurion in the form of a modified .50 Browning machine gun known as the ranging machine gun.

The experience gained so far, although limited, had shown that there were a number of very serious problems in connection with the gunnery on Conqueror. The majority of them could be related to problems with determining the correct range and to this end nothing could be achieved until the introduction of the Mk II rangefinder during the next training season. Other problems were centred on the performance of the HESH round. It was found that a standard correction of 200yd (183mm), which had been sufficient for the 20-pounder, fitted to Centurion, was proving too coarse for the 120mm to provide a second round hit on a 7ft-high (2m) target at 1,500yds (1,372m). Considering that the JS3 was only 2.44m high, that was not very encouraging.

Dispersion was also found to be greater than expected at ranges up to 2,250yd (2,057m), although it was hoped that more experience and training would help cure most of these problems. An assessment of the technique of shooting and gunnery drills had highlighted problems caused by the initial lack of training equipment and limited time available for individual crew training. The ridiculously small amount of 120mm ammunition available for gunnery training, the shortcomings of the Mk I rangefinder and the continual difficulty with the range-setting mechanism also caused problems. Even when the range-setting mechanism was working commanders were still passing the range to the gunner by means of the intercommunication system rather than trust the system; they also found it a lot quicker.

The relatively short time that individual vehicles had been off the road or the relatively few times they had failed to complete major exercises gave a slightly false impression that Conqueror was turning out to be a highly reliable vehicle. This did not take into account the high priority given to repairing Conqueror and the supply of spares that were available to support it. Things have not changed in contemporary times as the much-vaunted availability figures produced for Challenger I during the Gulf War show. The tank was available for most of the time due to the massive back-provided for it, with up to three power packs available for each MBT. Maj.-Gen. Rupert Smith has said that in the early days of training he was pleased if the formation could advance more than 2km without Challenger breaking down, so availability figures must always be looked at very carefully.

In spite of the problems noted above, however, Conqueror had shown that it could go where required, although road moves sometimes meant taking very circuitous routes which required a lot of planning and liaison with the local German authorities. This was felt will worth the trouble, as the tactical value of getting Conqueror to the battlefield was immense, although with the problems of the gunner having to wait for the gun to come back under his control after the vehicle had halted meant that Conqueror should never be the lead vehicle. The difficulty in trying to conceal Conqueror could be removed by digging in; this is still an excellent way of supplementing a vehicle's armour and was planned in any defence of Europe during the Cold War days. The disadvantage is the amount of time required to construct the pit for just one vehicle, and Royal Engineer resources will always be limited.

'A' Squadron 4th\7th Royal Dragoon Guards were nominated to carry out a digging-in trial with one Conqueror. The area chosen was on the NATO ranges at Hohne and took place between 27–29 July 1955. The ground was typical of the range's heathland and scattered scrub with mainly coniferous trees. The end result consisted of a pit 75ft (23m) long, which included a 35ft (11m) ramp, with a width of 14ft (4.3m) at the rear. The actual area occupied by the vehicle was 17ft (5m) wide as it was considered that maintenance would still be required, as vehicles could be in their pits for a long time if the situation deteriorated. With the vehicle in the pit and camouflaged and the surrounding area also camouflaged it was the perfect ambush position, except for one small point – it had taken 24 hours to construct and that did not take into account time taken for food and rest. In conclusion, if a vehicle could be placed into a pit this would be desirable from a defensive point of view, but against this had to be weighed the time taken and the fatigue induced in the crew.

Conquerors at rest, possibly at Hohne ranges. The left-hand tank has its engine decks up and radiators open while the right-hand one has only half the deck open. The vehicle between them is a Centurion ARV.

Conqueror at high speed on Soltau training area. Even at this close distance see how it is starting to blend in with its background even while moving.

4 Conqueror Described

Although many new features were introduced into Conqueror, its layout and construction followed the conventional British design in that the hull was split into three main compartments, these being the driver's compartment, the fighting compartment and the engine and transmission compartment.

THE HULL

The hull was of all-welded construction similar to Centurion, but in Conqueror the hull sides were vertical, unlike Centurion's which were inclined outwards as part of the design to help protect the vehicle from mine damage. It was felt that as Conqueror was not meant to be a leading vehicle the mine protection could be less than required for Centurion. Due to the large 80in (203cm) turret ring

it was necessary to build hull panniers which overhung the top run of the track.

The Driver's Compartment

The hull contains the driver's compartment, with the fighting compartment in the centre and the engine transmission compartment to the rear. A fireproof bulkhead separates the fighting and engine compartments. The driver's compartment is itself split into two separate sections. The driver is located in the right hand of the two sections, while the left-hand side is used as a stowage location for main armament ammunition. The driver sits on a seat, which is height adjustable to enable him to operate either with his head out of the tank, or with his hatch closed down. The driver's hatch, and in fact those of all the crew, were of a new design in

This shows the overhang required to accommodate the large turret ring. Also visible are the centre and rear stowage bins. To the left of the rear bin is the left-hand fuel filler. Author.

that they were of the lift-and-swing type as opposed to the normal British hatch that opened outwards. It was felt that the new-style hatch would enable the driver especially to be able to open his hatch to escape, regardless of the position of the turret, something that he could not do on Centurion. This type of hatch was designed to try to reduce the casualties caused by drivers trapped in a burning vehicle, as had happened so often during wartime. The driver could if required enter from the fighting compartment as well as through his hatch.

With the driver in his seat he had most of the

1 Instrument panel	15 Charging set indicator lamp
2 Revolution indicator	16 Charging set engine ignition switch
3 Fuel gauge	17 Charging set switchboard
4 Coolant temperature gauge	18 Generator reset switch
5 Panel lamp cover	19 Charging set engine starter switch
6 Speedometer	20 Charging set engine oil pressure
7 Instrument panel lamp switch	warning lamp
8 Main engine panel lamp switch	21 Exterior lighting switch
9 Driver's dual switchboard	22 Main engine starter switch
10 Bilge pump switch (not used)	23 Main engine oil pressure warning lamp
11 Driver's periscope wiper switch	24 Main engine switchboard
12 Main engine ignition switch	25 Priming pump switch box
13 Tail or convoy lamp change-over	26 Gun position indicator
switch	27 Fuel gauge change-over switch
14 Magneto test switch	

An extract from the official user handbook, showing the driver's switchboard and instrument panel, which was situated on his left-hand side. Crown copyright.

controls needed to operate the tank to hand. Forward of him and situated down by his feet were the clutch, brake and accelerator pedals arranged in the normal sequence as found in a car even though they were on a much larger scale. Further back and situated between his knees was the manually operated gear lever, which controlled the crash gearbox. There were no luxuries on this vehicle with every gear change of the double de-clutch method. This gave the driver five forward speeds and two reverse gears. The unwary driver could be caught out if he was not careful as there were two marks of gearbox, the Z52 and the Z52R, with the main difference as far as the driver was concerned being that the gears on the Z52R were laid out in the reverse of the Z52. So if not careful, problems could arise and instead of going forward after selecting first gear on the Z52 the driver could well find that instead of selecting first gear and moving forwards he had in fact selected reverse and was moving backwards, which could result in horrible consequences.

To his left and right were the steering levers,

1 Main brake drum R.H.
2 Steering brake drum R.H.
3 Breather, gearbox
4 Steering brake adjusters
5 Dipstick
6 Oil filter
7 Steering brake drum, L.H.

8 Gearbox output shaft coupling
9 Gearbox
10 Steering control rods
11 Gear control rods
12 Oil Filter
13 Main brake control rod

A view of the transmission compartment showing an unmodified gearbox; compare the location of the oil filler and filter on the modified gearbox. Crown copyright.

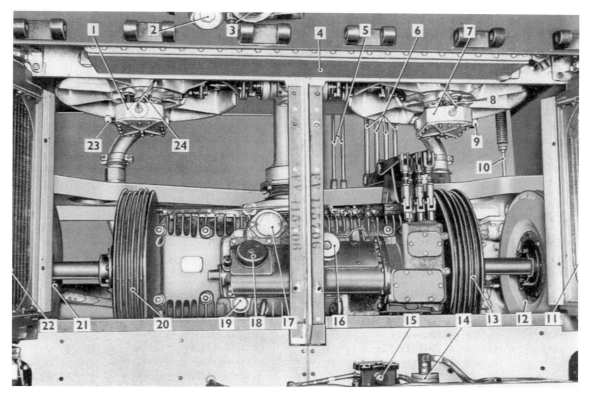

1 Oil box, L.H. fan
2 Filler, cooling system
3 Cover, cooling system filler
4 Header tank, cooling system
5 Steering control rods
6 Gear selector control rods
7 Oil box, R.H. fan
8 Breather, oil box
9 Filler, oil box
10 Main brakes control rod
11 R.H. radiator
12 R.H. main brake
13 R.H. steering brake
14 Trailer socket
15 Rear junction box and inspection lam socket
16 Oil filler
17 Oil Filler
18 Breather
19 Dipstick
20 L.H. steering brake
21 L.H. main brake
22 L.H. radiator
23 Filler, oil box
24 Breather, oil box

Views showing the layout of the modified gearbox – compare this with photo, p.68. Crown copyright.

which controlled the direction of travel of the tank. The steering levers replaced the conventional steering wheel as found in a car, thus to turn left the driver pulled the left stick and for right turns the right lever was pulled. In reverse the person guiding

the driver would indicate by hand signals which stick to pull, but this was reverse from going forwards. If the guide wished the back end of the tank to move to the left then the driver would be instructed to pull the left stick which made the back

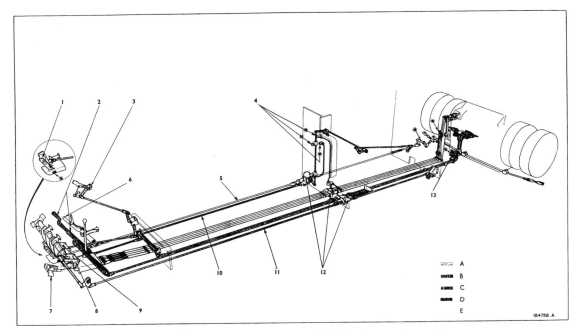

1 Accelerator edal
2 Steering levers
3 Hand throttle
4 Bulkhead guide lubricating nipples
5 Main brake operating rod
6 Parking brake lever
7 Clutch pedal check
8 Clutch pedal
9 Footbrake
10 Accelerator operating rod

11 Clutch operating rod
12 Bulkhead guides
13 Steering linkage cross-over
* Lubricating nipples
A Gear controls
B Accelerator controls
C Clutch controls
D Steering controls
E Main brake controls

Showing the layout of the controls within the hull. Notice the long run of the gear change rods. It can be seen that only a slight distortion over that length could have great problems. Crown copyright.

of the tank swing to the left although it was the right-hand side that was moving. This quirk of everything being reversed could cause some confusion to those new to tanks, when on trying to reverse they would hold up a hand and wonder why the tank went the opposite way, but it was a lesson soon learned. The turning circle was dependent on which gear was selected – for example, if in first gear the turning circle would only be 16ft (5m), but if fifth gear was used then the turning circle

increased to 140ft (43m). Also situated near the steering lever was the handbrake so great care had to be taken not to inadvertently apply the handbrake instead of the steering lever. Interlock was also fitted to prevent the driver applying both sticks at the same time.

Situated on the right-hand hull wall were all the controls for starting the main engine and also the auxiliary engine. The idea of having the controls for the latter in the driver's cab was an improvement

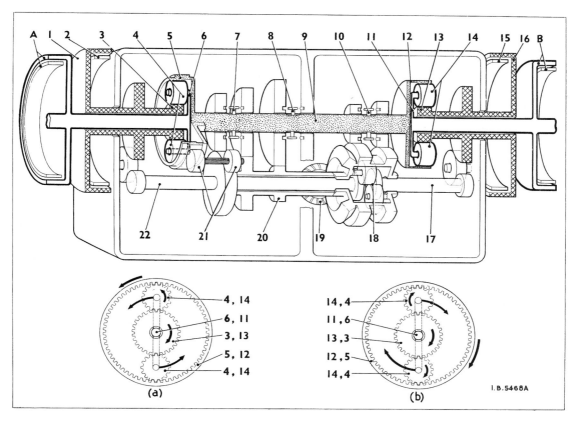

1 L.H. steering brake drum
2 L.H. steering brake
3 L.H. sun pinion
4 L.H. planet pinions
5 L.H. annulus
6 L.H. planet carrier and output shaft
7 2nd and 3rd gear dog
8 1st and low reverse gear dog
9 Layshaft
10 4th and 5th gear dog
11 R.H. planet carrier and output shaft
12 R.H. annulus

13 R.H. sun pinion
14 R.H. planet pinions
15 R.H. steering brake
16 R.H. steering brake drum
17 R.H. half shaft
18 Differential
19 Input pinion
20 Primary shaft
21 High reverse pinions
22 L.H. half shaft
A L.H. main brake assembly
B R.H. main brake assembly

(a) Epicyclic gears viewed from L.H. side showing action in forward gears
(b) Epicyclic gears viewed from L.H. side showing action in high reverse

For the more adventurous reader, a layout of the gear train within an unmodified gearbox. Crown copyright.

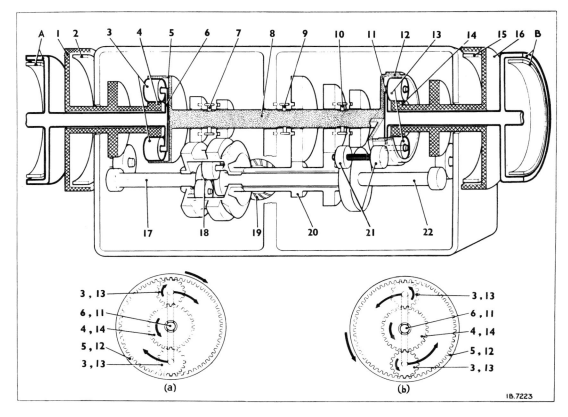

1 L.H. steering brake drum
2 L.H. steering brake
3 L.H. planet pinions
4 L.H. sun pinion
5 L.H. annulus
6 L.H. planet carrier and output shaft
7 2nd and 3rd gear dog
8 Layshaft
9 1st and low reverse gear dog
10 4th and 5th gear dog
11 R.H. planet carrier and output shaft
12 R.H. annulus
13 R.H. planet pinions
14 R.H. sun pinion

15 R.H. steering brake
16 R.H. steering brake drum
17 L.H. half shaft
18 Differential
19 Input pinion
20 Primary shaft
21 High reverse pinion
22 R.H. half shaft
 A L.H. main brake
 B R.H. main brake
(a) Epicyclic gears viewed from L.H. side
      showing action in forward gears
(b) Epicyclic gears viewed from L.H. side
      showing action in high reverse

Schematic of the inside of a modified gearbox. Crown copyright.

over the earlier marks of Centurion where the controls were situated on the bulkhead between the fighting compartment and the engine compartment. This meant that if you wished to run the auxiliary engine whilst static but had left the turret in the wrong position then it had to be traversed by hand until the controls could be reached. This was a very strenuous exercise and not to be recommended often. Obviously with the control in the driver's cab it was much easier either to climb into or lean in and start the auxiliary engine. The cab also contained the normal instrumentation that one would expect such as a speedometer, rev counter and everything that the driver would require to monitor the condition of both engines. When operating closed down the driver could see by means of three periscopes on the Mk I and only one on the Mk II, which was considered a retrograde step and was heavily criticized in the trial report, but no change was made.

The reason for this was that it had been found that the three-periscope hull roof design had in fact created a weak joint in the armour. By only providing one periscope this allowed the designers to make the hull roof horizontal on the Mk II instead of the more sloped roof on the Mk I, thus making a better join with the glacis plate and creating better protection. This however, was never explained to the user, leaving them continually raising the same point about periscopes without receiving a satisfactory answer.

To the driver's left was stowage for 25 brass charges for the main armament, which would form the basis for replenishing the ready rounds in the turret. This was a task that obviously would have to be carried out whilst the vehicle was static. To the rear behind the driver's seat was the location for the four 6-volt vehicle batteries; also in the cab were the two CO_2 bottles for the fixed fire-fighting system. This system could be activated either from within the driver's cab or from two handles situated in tunnels within the front left and right stowage bins. Entry and exit for the driver was normally through the driver's hatch, but with the gun in certain positions he could crawl through into the fighting compartment. It had been decided not to provide an escape hatch, as could be found on most American tanks and Russian. The official view was that by putting an escape hatch into the belly armour of a vehicle you would weaken the already thin armour there, which, providing that you are not the driver trapped in there, is a reasonable argument.

If we were describing a normal British vehicle of the time, such as Centurion, it would be the normal

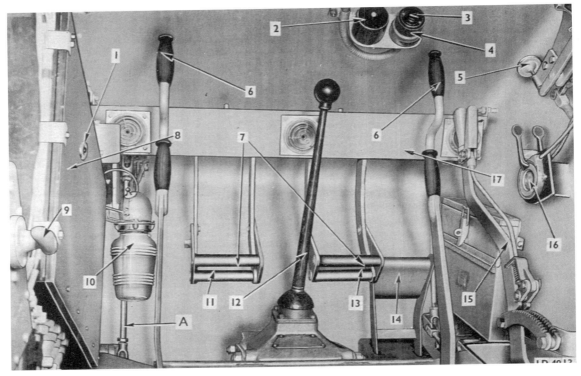

1 Generator reset switch
2 Cover
3 Horn button
4 Diswitch
5 Hand throttle control
6 Steering levers
7 Pedal adators
8 Generator anel
9 Battery master switch

10 Driver's eriscoe object rism sray
11 Clutch edal
12 Gear lever
13 Brake pedal
14 Accelerator
15 Handbrake lever
16 Charging set engine controls
17 Air duct
A Adjustment rod for clutch edal free travel

Sketch showing the driver's foot and hand controls. Of interest is the size of the gear stick and on the base of the stick mounting can be seen a plate showing the gear locations. Crown copyright.

practice to say that the remainder of the crew were situated in the turret. This, as we have seen. was not quite true of Conqueror, as although the remaining three crew members were in the turret, the commander was isolated in his FCT. This was the only time that this layout has been used on a British tank. However, the gunner and loader occupied the traditional locations for their jobs.

The Gunner and Loader

The gunner was situated on the right of the gun with easy access to all of his gun controls. On his right-hand side mounted on the turret ring is his power control handle for power traverse. Situated to his left and forward is the elevation power control, which meant that whilst the gunner was using full

The driver's hatch on a Mk I Conqueror. It can be seen from this shot how much more vision the driver had with the three periscopes compared to the later one only on the Mk II. Author.

Showing the large standard headlights fitted to all versions of Conqueror. Notice the very neat join of the glacis plate. Author.

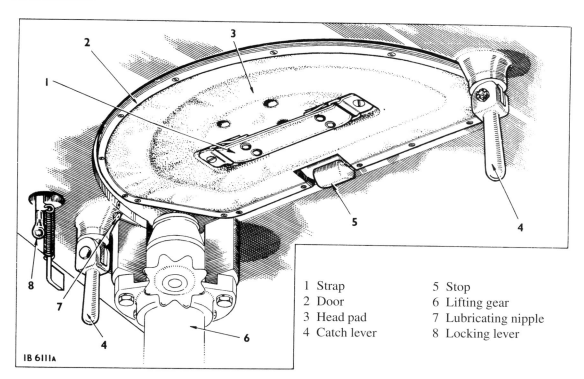

1 Strap   5 Stop
2 Door   6 Lifting gear
3 Head pad   7 Lubricating nipple
4 Catch lever   8 Locking lever

Handbook drawing of the various components of the driver's hatch on late production vehicles.

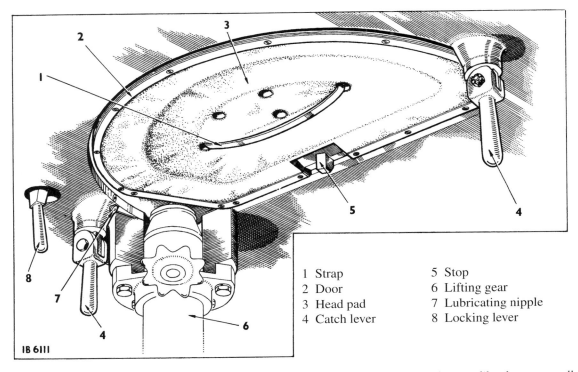

1	Strap	5	Stop
2	Door	6	Lifting gear
3	Head pad	7	Lubricating nipple
4	Catch lever	8	Locking lever

IB 6111

Another handbook shot showing the early pattern hatch. Although at first glance they both seem alike, there are small differences and small changes will occur throughout a vehicle's life.

Showing the gunner's controls including the power traverse and elevation controls. Notice how the power traverse controller is offset. Crown copyright.

1 Hand traverse handle   2 Power traverse controller   3 Turntable drive bracket

power both his hands were needed to control the turret and main armament. Today, things are more civilized with Challenger II using a small rubber-covered button which combines both movements in the manner of a computer game pad.

The traverse controller handle is known as a spade grip mainly because it resembles the handle of a garden spade, and built into this handle is a lever known as a grip switch; if this was not depressed when the gunner held the handle then no power traverse could take place. To use the power equipment the gunner had to ensure that all the gun control equipment was switched on and running. Before moving, the turret under power it was essential to make sure that the driver was not trying to climb in or out of his hatch, or attempting to move from his cab into the turret. Checks on the vehicle had to include a check that no bin lids had

been left open, that the engine decks were closed and that there were no obstructions internally or externally. Failure to observe these checks could result in damage to the vehicle or worse still to personnel.

Once the gunner was happy that movement of the gun would not injure the driver or anyone else and there were no obstructions he could use power traverse and elevation. The gunner had to place his right hand onto the controller making sure that he squeezed the grip switch, with the gun-control equipment running, then when he inclined the controller either left or right the turret would move in that direction. The further he inclined the controller the faster the turret would traverse until the maximum speed of one complete rotation of the turret in 24 seconds was achieved. The turret would come to a dead stop on the grip switch being

A well-corroded power traverse controller pictured in a hard target on Salisbury Plain, now in the author's collection and restored. Author.

released. The commander's controller for his FCT was similar to the gunner's, but with the addition of a further switch on top of the spade grip to enable him to override the gunner.

It was not always possible to use powered laying equipment, possibly due to the tactical situation when no engines were running, or due to a breakdown of the equipment. In cases such as this, the gunner was provided with the means of hand traverse and elevation. The gunner had either an elevating hand wheel or a handle depending on the mark of vehicle. These were both connected to a hydraulic pump, which was connected by means

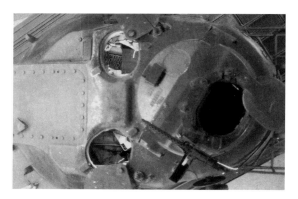

A good aerial view looking down into the commander's, gunner's and loader's hatches. Notice the lift-and-swing type hatches on all three locations. Author.

1 Gunner's leg shield
2 Gunner's seat
3 Emergency/run lever

The power traverse emergency/run control lever. This was used as a last resort if power to the turret failed. By moving this lever a fixed rate of traverse was provided by the vehicle batteries, but only for a limited time. A similar system was employed on Centurion and Chieftain. Crown copyright.

of flexible tubing to a hydraulic motor mounted on the elevation gearbox. The motor was connected to the main shaft of the gearbox by means of a dog clutch, which was disengaged electrically when power was switched on. The gunner also had situated close at hand all the controls that he needed to control lighting, armament selection and sight wipers and washers. He sat on a seat that was adjustable for height only and his means of entry and exit to the turret were by his own hatch of a similar design to the driver's. The gunner's hatch was situated immediately above him, which in itself was an unusual feature for a British tank and was brought about by the inclusion of the FCT which took the place of the traditional commander's cupola that used to be the gunner's way in and out. This hatch allowed the gunner to be able to stand on his seat and look out of the vehicle. In tanks with the more traditional layout the gunner cannot easily get out if the commander is standing in the cupola. This feature of the gunner being able to look out of the vehicle did help to alleviate feelings of claustrophobia, which gunners can sometimes feel if they are left in that position all day long.

In an emergency, the perspex safety shield to the gunner's left could be removed and he could try to crawl across the gun and out of the loader's hatch; obviously this was not a recommended course of action if the gun kit was running!

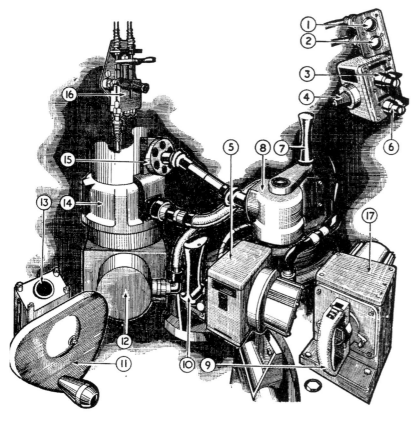

Drawing from the gunnery handbook showing nearly all the gunner's controls and also how cramped it could be in that location. Crown copyright.

1. Firing circuit warning lamp
2. Tank movement warning lamp
3. Alternator switch
4. Elevation trim switch
5. Elevation controller
6. Metadyne switch
7. Manual traverse handle
8. Hand traverse gear
9. Spade grip traverse controller
10. Handle elevation controller
11. Hand elevating wheel
12. Tachometer generator
13. Oil reservoir
14. Traverse gear box
15. Hand traverse gear
16. Selector mechanical firing gear
17. Traverse controller

However, it might be necessary if the vehicle was hit or damaged.

The loader was situated on the left of the turret and had more freedom of movement than the rest of the crew, in that he could at least move around whilst carrying out his various jobs. His two main tasks were the loading of both the 120mm and the .30 Browning machine gun. He would also be required to carry out any gun drills required to keep both weapons operational. On top of this the loader was also the tank's radio operator. He would be required to look after the radios that were carried in the rear of the turret. These could be the WS 19, WS 88 AFV, WS 31 AFV, C12, C42 or the B47. The exact radio fit would very much depend on the year of service of the tank. As well as being responsible

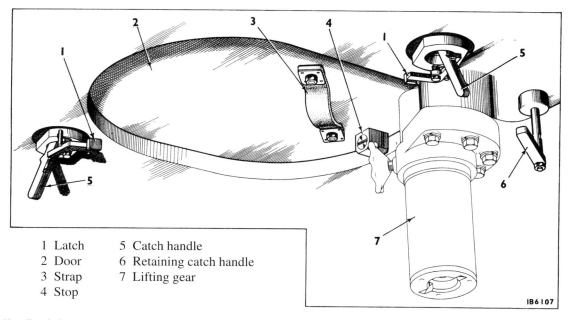

1	Latch	5	Catch handle
2	Door	6	Retaining catch handle
3	Strap	7	Lifting gear
4	Stop		

Handbook drawings showing the inside detail of the gunner's access hatch. Notice the size of the pillar required to support the lift-and-swing type hatches. Crown copyright.

for tuning in the radio and keeping it on the frequency required, he would also have to take down most of the radio messages and decipher any codes. This was of great help to the vehicle commander, allowing him to concentrate on commanding the vehicle efficiently knowing that he could rely on the operator for any grid references or a tactical update. This situation has not changed a great deal for tank crews today even with the onset of technology.

That was the official allocation of the loader's tasks, but as far as the crew were concerned there was one other duty that the loader had to carry out by virtue of the fact that situated at his station was the socket for the boiling vessel. This in its form as used on Conqueror and Centurion was nothing more than a saucepan fitted with a boiling element. However, it was a valuable aid for morale, giving the crew the means to be able to have a hot meal or drink more or less as they pleased. The poor infantry did not have such luxuries and were forced to try to light a hexamine tablet and boil water in a

mess tin, not much fun with the wind howling and the rain lashing down. However, the boiling vessel could only safely be used when the gun was facing the 12 o'clock location and ideally the vehicle should be static.

However, when the annual gunnery camp came round the loader really had to start earning his pay, as although the vehicle could only carry 30 rounds of main armament ammunition it was, as we have already seen, of the split nature with the brass case for the charge weighing 43lb (19kg), the APDS projectile 21lb (9.5kg) and HE\HESH 35lb (16kg). Added to this was the task of keeping out of the way of the recoiling gun and having to load the co-ax machine gun and carry out the stoppage drills on it, all the while being shouted at by the commander at the top of his voice. Alternatively, a loader could be unlucky and fall foul of one of the gunnery instructors who would be sitting on the turret for some of the shoots. It can be seen that at least for a fortnight of a year the loader had to work very hard.

The loader's side of the turret had stowage for

Another view of the hatches. If you look carefully you can see the power controls inside the gunner's hatch and part of the breech through the loader's.

seven main armament rounds in ready containers, six boxes of .30 Browning ammunition with one stowed in the ready tray and five more under the radio sets. Also stowed on the loader's side would be various small arms ammunition, such as 9mm for the crew sten guns, thirty-six Mills hand grenades, fuses for the smoke grenades fired from dischargers fitted either side of the turret and various tools to maintain the weapons. Coupled with all this were

various items of personnel kit and the worst seat on the vehicle as it was expected that the loader would be on his feet most of the time, so he would not need such a comfortable seat as the remainder of the crew.

For the remainder of the year though, the loader would help out with the rest of the crew to complete all the many tasks that were required to keep something as complex as Conqueror mobile. These

Probably the most important piece of equipment on board – the electric boiling vessel. Once plugged in, using the cable to the right in the drawing several pints of boiling water could be swiftly made. This was far easier than trying to light a petrol cooker or hexamine block cooker outside in the rain. The boiling vessel still survives in a much more modified form and is still a prized part of a vehicle's equipment.

81

would include the major job of changing the tracks which would happen at least once a training season. It was a complete crew task and some troops even made it a troop task, which really made the job a lot easier.

The Commander

The final member of the crew was the vehicle commander and, as we have seen already it was felt that he should be at least an SNCO and have attended the long instructor's course at the RAC Gunnery School at Lulworth. However, this did not always work out and in the end it was never followed through to the level that the powers that be would have liked. The main reason for this was that the units could not spare enough men to attend a course for two-and-a-half months away from the unit. The occupancy of the commander's seat was therefore left very much up to individual units to sort out. This was also dependent on how the unit had organized the Conquerors within the framework of the Centurion troops. For example, if the Conqueror was the fourth tank in a Centurion troop it would be more than likely be commanded by a full corporal, but if the Conqueror was organized into a troop then it would be commanded the same as a normal tank troop, i.e. officer, sergeant or corporal.

However, regardless of who commanded the vehicle, their task was identical, for as commander they were responsible for the vehicle and the crew and for ensuring that both were ready at all times. When they were in the field the commander had more to worry about, as it was his job to ensure that the vehicle moved tactically from bound to bound. Ensuring that they were not seen by the enemy was no easy task with the gunner not having total control of Conqueror's gun kit. He also had to map read, control the other three members of the crew, ensure that he was always listening to the radio, as one sure way to make yourself unpopular with the squadron leader was to miss his messages to you. If you did, it would usually result in a summons to his tank that night for an interview without coffee.

To help the commander in this task he was for the first time situated in a separate fire-control turret. The main reason for this was to enable the fitting of a rangefinder to enable accurate ranges to be found for the first time. Prior to this, the commander had usually estimated the range or he worked it out from a map. Neither method was particularly accurate, especially for a tank that was meant to achieve a first round hit at long range. The FCT was a one-piece casting, with the commander's hatch situated to the rear centre, and the 47in (119cm) rangefinder running across the turret occupying the centre part. On either side of the FCT were armoured covers operated from inside to protect the rangefinding heads. Also fitted on the right-hand side was a mounting for the commander's .30 Browning machine gun, which could be operated from inside the turret to give the commander some protection. The commander's hatch could be left open, fully closed or locked in a position known as the umbrella position, which allowed him some overhead cover whilst still being able to have his head above the level of the turret.

The FCT was power-operated and could traverse 360 degrees independently of the main turret, but strangely no provision was ever made for hand traverse to be fitted. This was one of the recommendations from the trials, as it was felt necessary to have a back-up if power was not available.

The inside of the FCT was very cramped, particularly once the commander had stowed all his personal kit such as binoculars, waterproof coat, maps and the machine gun ammunition. With one box in the feed tray for the .30 Browning, one box on the floor to the left of the commander's seat and two boxes on the floor right of the commander's seat the space soon became very full. The commander had a spade grip similar to the gunner's, but also the facility to override the gunner if required. On the commander's controller was a switch which when pressed would line up the main turret with the FCT.

On the ranges, the commander would be responsible for taking all the ranges using the FCT

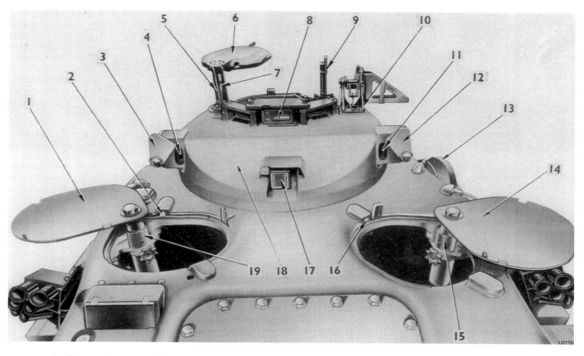

1 Gunner's access door
2 Catch, gunner's access door
3 Cover, rangefinder aperture
4 Rangefinder aperture
5 Commander's door stop
6 Commander's access door
7 Release lever
8 Sight, M.G.
9 Bracket, strut
10 MG mounting

11 Rangefinder aperture
12 Cover, rangefinder aperture
13 Cable reel
14 Operator's access door
15 Lifting gear
16 Catch, operator's access door
17 Sight, main armament
18 Fire control turret
19 Lifting gear

A very good drawing from the handbook showing all the hatches and mounting detail, sights and smoke dischargers. Crown copyright.

range finder and applying them to the main armament. His job was to select the targets to engage and the type of ammunition with which to engage it, and then issue the correct fire order to the crew. Having done all that he would then control the gunner in the shoot and if necessary step in and give corrections if he thought that the gunner had not got it right quite. A Centurion commander had tended to improve his gunner's aim by the tried-and-trusted

Gunnery School solution of a well-aimed kick, but as the Conqueror commander was isolated in the FCT he had to make do with a few choice words.

To really make the commander's day would be the total failure of the Mollins gear, which meant he would have to resort to winding the system manually, not the best of things on a hot summer's day on the Hohne ranges. The times for this, as we have seen earlier, would not make for a speedy

Looking down into the fire control turret of the Tank Museum's Mk I Conqueror. Notice the round dial with a rectangle and two lines on it on the right of the picture. This is the commander's gun position indicator and it can be illuminated and is also luminous. It enables the commander to see the location of the main gun and his FCT when fully closed down as both pointers move in relationship to the representation of the hull. Tank Museum.

Another view inside the Bovington Conqueror. Visible in the centre of the picture is the no. 8 sight with its two eyepieces. Above this is the no. 6 sight which is used for firing the .30 Browning machine gun. To the left of these is the eyepiece for the rangefinder, and to the left is the power traverse controller with the switch on top for line up of the FCT with the main turret. The commander seat is at the bottom of the picture and situated in front of that is the FCT rotary base junction. Tank Museum.

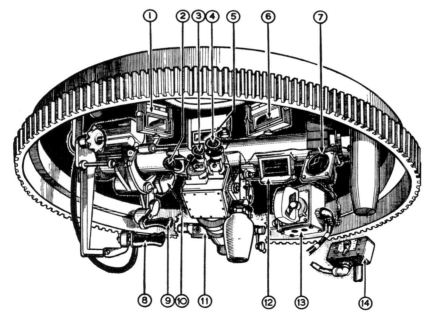

1. Episcope
2. Rangefinder eyepiece
3. Range scale eyepiece
4. Telescope eyepiece
5. Periscope sighting No. 6
6. Episcope
7. Gun and turret position indicator
8. MG firing handle
9. Rangefinder elevation controller
10. Magslip transmitter unit No. 5
11. Collimator
12. Rangefinder working head
13. Traverse controller
14. Range adjustment unit (range setter)

Gunnery handbook drawing of the layout and names of the various components that make up the FCT. Crown copyright.

shoot; also it would distract the commander from his prime task of commanding the tank.

THE ENGINE AND TRANSMISSION COMPARTMENTS

So far, we have covered the crew and the main armament. Now we move on to the rear of the vehicle and to the engine and transmission compartments. These occupy the rear portion of the hull and contain the main engine, an auxiliary engine, the gearbox, steering and main brakes. Access to the compartment was via seven louvred engine decks and seven transmission decks, which were interlocking and could only be opened in the correct sequence, numbering from right to left 1, 2, 3, 4, 5, 6, 7.

Depending on the mark of the vehicle, various small access points were fitted to the main engine decks to allow for the topping up of coolant, fuel or engine oil without the need to raise all the decks. The main engine itself was a derivative of the famous Merlin used on the Spitfire but suitably derated and modified for installation into AFVs and called Meteor. This had first been used successfully in the Comet and Cromwell during World War II. It was further refined in Centurion. Conqueror was fitted with an M120, no.2 Mk IA, liquid-cooled petrol engine developing approximately 810bhp at 2,800rpm. The main difference between the Centurion engine and Conqueror's was that the latter had been fitted with a fuel-injection system whereas Centurion's was equipped with a conventional carburettor system. Fitting a fuel-injection system gave Conqueror more bhp and around 1.5mph better performance than Centurion. Fuel tanks containing 221 gallons (1,005litres) of 80-octane petrol were situated either side of the engine compartment and as a general figure fuel consumption worked out at about 0.43 mpg for road work and 0.27 to .33 mpg for cross-country work.

To provide electrical power for the vehicle the main engine drove a generator which provided 150 amps over a speed range of 3,300 to 8,400rpm. This produced electrical power for the vehicle and also charged the four 6 volt, 115Ah batteries situated behind the driver's seat. During the war, the only way to keep batteries fully charged had been either to keep the engine running all the time or have some vehicles carry a small petrol generator that could be rigged during quiet moments to charge the system. Neither of these was the ideal solution, as leaving the main engine running was not tactically acceptable and was a serious drain on fuel, and having to unpack and set up the portable generator proved not to be a pleasant occupation, especially in a hurried move out in the dark. In view of this, the British allowed space in the new designs for a generator to be provided that was powered by another engine but one which was not much bigger than the average car engine. In Conqueror's case it was a four-cylinder, liquid-cooled, side valve petrol engine which could develop 29bhp at 3,000 rpm. In conjunction with the generator it provided 350A at 28.5V continuously, thus allowing the vehicle to run all the electrical services it would need, such as the power traverse and boiling vessel, without the need for the main engine.

The aux. gen., as it is more commonly known to tank crews, is very quiet, unlike Chieftain's; you have to have experienced this vehicle's early-morning call of the revs building up to operating speed truly to appreciate the difference in noise. The idea of the aux gen has now become standard British tank design practice. It is interesting to note that after their Gulf experience the Americans are now providing the M1 Abrams with its own generator system, although as it is basically an afterthought it has had to be fixed to the back of the vehicle in its own armoured box. This is not the best place for it, but having designed the engine compartment to take the gas turbine no space was left for what was thought at the time an unnecessary item. The gas turbine, however, has proved to be a thirsty engine and any period that it can be closed down is a major saving in fuel. The aux. gen. shares the same fuel and cooling system as the main engine but has its own oil supply. With the main engine, aux. gen. and two fuel tanks the engine compartment is very cramped as the

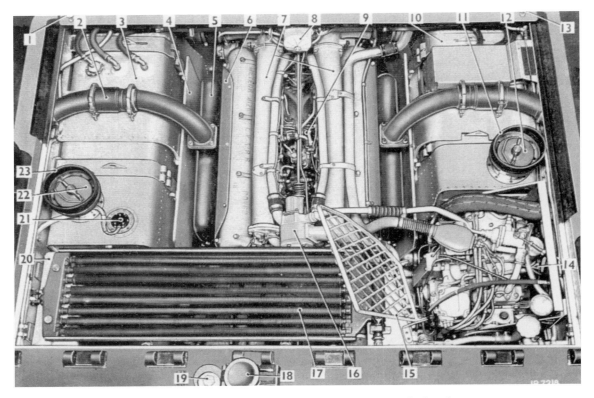

1 Breather, R.H. fuel tank
2 Exhaust pipe, left bank
3 L.H. fuel tank, large
4 Heat shield, L.H. fuel tank
5 Exhaust manifold, left bank
6 Heat shield, engine
7 Air intake pipes
8 Fuel tap and filter
9 Fuel injection pump
10 R.H. fuel tank
11 Flexible splash guard
12 Filler, R.H. fuel tank
13 Breather, L.H. fuel tank
14 Charging set engine
15 Guard, charging set engine
16 Thermostat
17 Oil cooler
18 Cover, cooling system filler
19 Filler, cooling system
20 L.H fuel tank, small
21 Tank unit, fuel gauge
22 Filler, L.H. fuel tank
23 Flexible splash guard

Handbook views of the engine compartment. Note how the Meteor and the fuel tanks fill the compartment. Crown copyright.

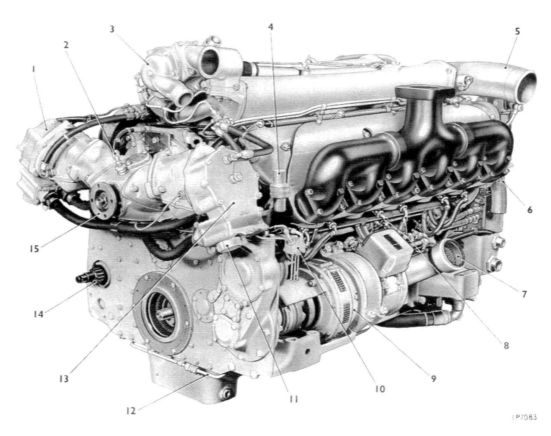

1P7083

1 Magneto, L.H.
2 Magneto and fan drive lubrication pipe
3 Thermostat housing
4 Modification certificate holder
5 Air intake pipe, 'A' bank
6 Flame detector (obsolescent type shown)
7 Generator air cooling pipe
8 Sparkling plugs, 'A' bank (exhaust side)

9 Generator
10 Flame detector (obsolescent type shown)
11 Ignition harness protection cap
12 Generator drive lubrication pipe
13 Magneto, R.H.
14 Starter motor pinion
15 Fan drive coupling

Three-quarter view of the Rolls Royce Meteor engine. Even from this handbook drawing the size of this unit is apparent. Crown copyright.

1 Secondary fuel filter
2 Main oil filters
3 Air intake throttle linkage
4 Air intake pipes
5 Fuel injection pump oil filter
6 Oil pressure switch
7 Booster coil (ignition)
8 Flame detector (obsolescent type shown)
9 Thermostat housing
10 Magneto, L.H.
11 Flame detector (obsolescent type shown)
12 Starter motor
13 Sparkling plugs, 'B' bank (exhaust side)
14 Oil pressure relief valve
15 Coolant pump inlet, L.H.
16 Fuel pump, L.H.
17 Oil inlet pipe to pressure pump
18 Cylinder jacket drain pipe, 'B' bank
19 Oil pressure pump
20 Oil scavenge filter housings
21 Oil scavenge pump
22 Fuel pump, R.H.
23 Electrical junction boxes
24 Engine revolution counter
25 Coolant pump inlet, R.H.

Another view, this time showing the three-quarter front left. Notice where the spark plugs are situated, compare that with the view in fig. 78 and imagine the poor fitter having to change those and the other side with the engine in situ – a notoriously long and awkward job. Crown copyright.

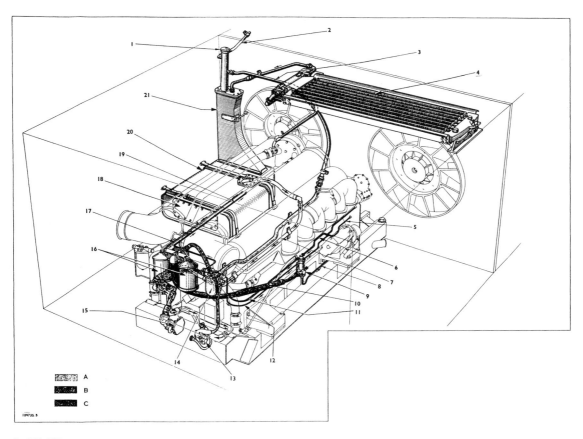

1 Oil filler cap
2 Breather pipe
3 Engine breather pipe
4 Oil cooler
5 Feed to auxiliary drive gears
6 Feed to magneto and fan drive gears
7 Suction pipe, tank to pressure pump
8 Feed to generator drive
9 Relief valve
10 Delivery pipe, filters to relief valve
11 Feed to wheelcase
12 Feed to filter for fuel injection pump
13 Pressure pump
14 Fuel injection pump oil filter
15 Scavenge pump
16 Oil filters
17 Return pipe, fuel injection pump to wheelcase
18 Oil tank inspection cover
19 Feed from filter to fuel injection pump
20 Oil tank
21 Fothing tower
A High pressure
B Return
C Low pressure

Again a handbook shot, this time showing the lubrication system. It can be seen here that there is no sump as in a car engine; instead there is a separate oil tank, which is to help keep the height of the vehicle down. This is known as a dry sump system. Crown copyright.

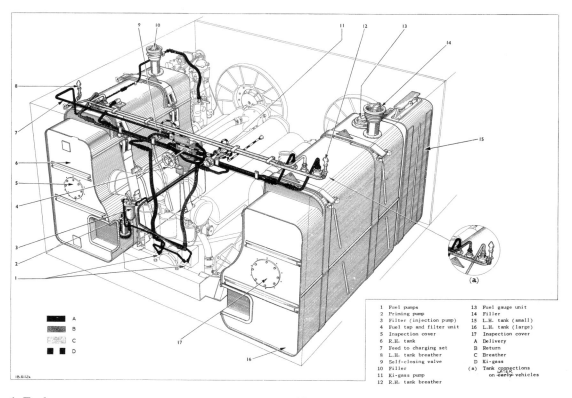

1	Fuel pumps	13	Fuel gauge unit
2	Priming pump	14	Filler
3	Filter (injection pump)	15	L.H. tank (small)
4	Fuel tap and filter unit	16	L.H. tank (large)
5	Inspection cover	17	Inspection cover
6	R.H. tank	A	Delivery
7	Feed to charging set	B	Return
8	L.H. tank breather	C	Breather
9	Self-closing valve	D	Ki-gass
10	Filler	(a)	Tank connections
11	Ki-gass pump		on ~~early~~ vehicles
12	R.H. tank breather		

1 Fuel pumps
2 Priming pump
3 Filter (injection pump)
4 Fuel tap and filter unit
5 Inspection cover
6 R.H. tank
7 Feed to charging set
8 L.H. tank breather
9 Self-closing valve
10 Filler
11 Ki-gass pump

12 R.H. breather
13 Fuel gauge unit
14 Filler
15 L.H. tank (small)
16 L.H. tank (large)
17 Inspection cover
 A Delivery
 B Return
 C Breather
 D Di-gass
(a) Tank connections on later vehicles

This shows the layout of the fuel system and again the most obvious feature is the size of the petrol tanks on either side of the Meteor. Crown copyright.

The vehicle batteries housed behind the driver's seat. Batteries are the most neglected item in AFV servicing, generally due to the awkward location in which they are usually placed. Crown copyright.

was felt that the vehicle's weight and extra suspension unit would take up any shocks. Of interest, the Caernarvon was fitted with shock absorbers on its front and rear units and they were only removed upon those vehicles' conversion to Conqueror. A major departure for the British was the use of resilient steel-rimmed road wheels, instead of the more usual rubber tyres. These wheels have a steel outside rim with a replaceable rubber inner tyre enclosed inside. This was meant to improve the life of the wheel, but in fact it just created more servicing for the crew and in practice a new wheel was more often than not obtained and fitted rather than the old one stripped down. This

picture shows, and it was something of a nightmare for REME to try to work on some of the components *in situ*.

Other problems that occurred with the engine compartment were again due to the notion of some COs that if you were a tank crewman then it did not matter what tank it was. So some Centurion drivers suddenly found themselves trying to understand the workings of the fuel-injection system, and where on earth were the fanbelts? Tpr Parsons of 3 RTR remembers standing on the back decks looking without success for the fan belts, until it was pointed out that Conqueror did not have them as the fans were driven mechanically when the main engine was running and electrically when only the aux. gen. was running.

One major modification that took place has almost become legend in the RAC and certainly features in a well-known song that concerned the individual regiment and was based on the fact that the gearbox was in but upside down. Things were not quite that bad but a great deal of confusion was caused when the Z52 gearbox was replaced with the Z52R; earlier internal modifications had indeed produced a gearbox that was back to front.

The Conqueror's suspension system followed the pattern of Centurion except for having one extra wheel station. The method of springing was the tried and tested Horstman system, however unlike Centurion no shock absorbers had been fitted as it

This shows the auxiliary generator engine that was used to supply power to the electrical services on the vehicle without the need for running the main engine. It is painted in different colours due to the fact that it was an instructional model and each colour represents a particular system. Author.

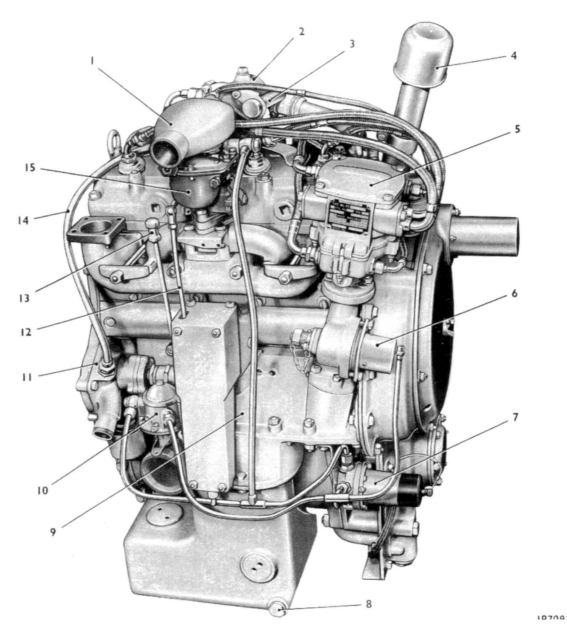

1 Air intake pipe
2 Thermostat housing
3 Modification certificate holder
4 Engine oil filler cap and breather
5 Distributor
6 Engine revolution recorder
7 Electrical fuel pump
8 Oil drain pipe connection
9 Governor housing
10 Mechanical fuel pump
11 Coolant pump
12 Governor to carburetter control rod
13 Oil level dipstick
14 Thermostat by-pass pipe
15 Carburetter

Left-hand side view of the charging engine. Crown copyright.

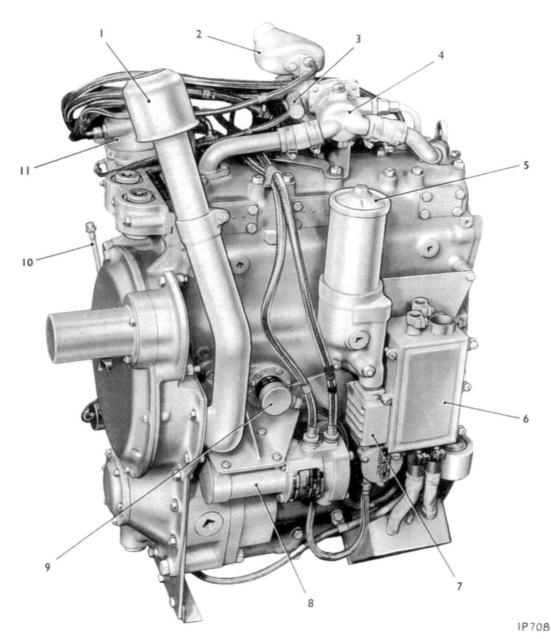

IP708

1 Engine oil filler cap and breather
2 Air intake pipe
3 Modification certificate holder
4 Thermostat housing
5 Oil filter
6 Electrical junction box
7 Ballast resistance box
8 Ignition coil
9 Oil pressure switch
10 Fuel inlet pipe
11 Distributor

Right-hand view of the charging engine. Crown copyright.

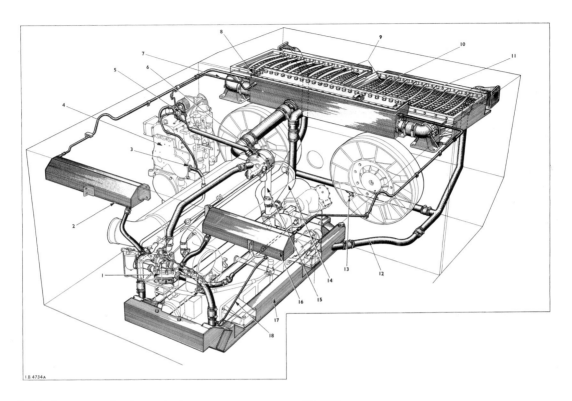

1 Coolant pump (main engine)
2 R.H. subsidiary header tank
3 Coolant pump (charging set engine)
4 Charging set engine
5 Thermostat (charging set engine)
6 Thermostat (main engine)
7 Balance pipe
8 Pressure relief valve
9 Radiators

10 Filler cap
11 Header tank
12 Radiator outlet pipe
13 Drain tap
14 Header tank by-pass pipe
15 Thermostat by-pass pipe
16 L.H. subsidiary header tank
17 Engine mounting and coolant rail
18 Cylinder drain pipe

The layout of the vehicle cooling system. When you look at this it is worthwhile comparing it to the layout in your own car and you then realize how simple your car system is compared to that employed by AFVs. Crown copyright.

also proved to be the quickest method of replacing damaged wheels.

In the location of the idler wheels and final drive sprockets Conqueror was rather more traditional, with the idler mounted at the front and the sprocket at the rear. Drive was taken from the engine via a 16in (406mm) triple plate dry clutch to the gearbox

and from the gearbox out to the sprockets. These were fitted with two removable sprocket rings either side which engaged into the track and thus moved the vehicle. Reduction at the sprockets was for the Z52 box 9.895 to 1 and for the Z52R 10.668 to 1. The vehicle ran on cast manganese steel track 31in (788mm) wide. A full set consisted of 102

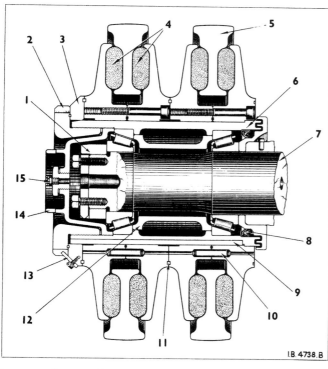

1 Axle nut
2 Hub nut
3 Locking ring
4 Rubber tyres
5 Steel tyre
6 Hub sleeve
7 Axle arm
8 Oil seal
9 Key
10 Dowel
11 Seal
12 Distance piece
13 Locking plate
14 Hub cap
15 Lubricating nipple

A very good section through a road wheel. Of note are the rubber tyres surrounded by the steel tyre. Crown copyright.

This shows very well the make-up of the suspension unit. This unit has been driven over the ramp 4 and it has compressed the springs in the unit, allowing the leading wheel to rise. It was then locked into position by means of the strut 2. The vehicle then was moved off the ramp, which left the wheel in a raised and freely rotating position. This would then allow the REME to check the wheel station for such things as rim rock. Crown copyright.

1 Axle arm   2 Strut   3 Rebound bracket   4 Ramp

95

links when new, reducing to ninety-seven when the REME were asked to examine with a view to replacement.

Adjustment of each track was carried out by the movement of an eccentric axle mounted at the front of the vehicle. The inner end of the axle pivoted in a bracket mounted on the hull plate. The outer end carried the idler wheel. Rotation of the eccentric axle altered the track tension. The vehicle was also provided with four top rollers per side which supported the top run of the track, one roller being secured to spindles on each suspension unit. This suspension system in fact gave a very comfortable ride, partly due to the extra suspension unit and partly to the very wide track; stories abound of Conqueror managing to get into areas that the Centurion crews would never dare to venture.

Externally, Conqueror was equipped with three

A view of the massive and very heavy sprocket. Four of these are used two to each hub. During use the teeth wear very quickly and a check needs to be kept on them. Like brakes on a car, when you change one you change them all. Crown copyright.

stowage bins either side – for greater details of the contents of these bins see the stowage drawings at the end of the book. The front right and left bins had locations built in for access to the handles that controlled the fire extinguisher system fitted into the engine compartment. This consisted of two 7lb (3kg) CO_2 extinguishers fitted to the rear of the driver's cab with piping running through the fighting compartment into the engine compartment. Flame detectors in the engine compartment would set off an audible alarm which could also be heard in the crew's radio headsets, thus alerting them to a fire. They could then pull the handles and set off the extinguishers. The two handles in the front bins allowed the operation of the extinguisher bottles from a safe distance as the effects of CO_2 are none too pleasant.

Situated on the front and rear of the vehicle are the normal head, side and tail lights normally found on most vehicles, although military vehicles have one extra light that would not be found on an average car. In the centre of the rear hull is a small light that shines downwards and is used for night driving when no other lights are permitted. Following this convoy light on an undulating expanse of ground calls for great skill and concentration by the driver as the light produced is not very great. The feeling of despair when the light does not reappear where expected has to be experienced to be understood.

The bins contained the tools and personal kit of the crew. The aforementioned Tpr Parsons remembered his tool kit: 'the tool kit itself was absolutely magnificent and I had to occasionally cover mine in grease and grit so that it would not look quite so good and subsequently get nicked.' Various other items such as shovels, crowbars and so on were stowed on the catwalks themselves along with four spare track links.

The rear of the vehicle had situated on the left-hand side an armoured box into which a standard issue first-aid box was fitted and below it the infantry tank telephone. This was a telephone handset by which anyone on the ground could, by opening the armoured door and pulling out the

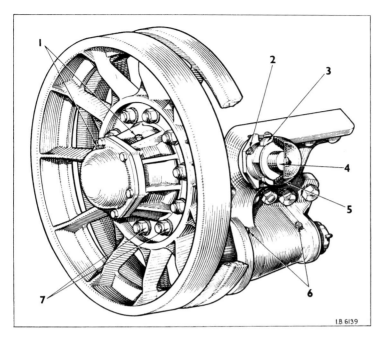

1 Wheel lubricating nipples
2 Adjusting nut lubricating nipple
3 Locking plate
4 Adjusting screw
5 Gaiter
6 Eccentric axle lubricating nipples
7 Wheel nuts

To enable the track to be kept at the correct tension on tracked vehicles an adjustable wheel is fitted, known as the idler wheel. Sometimes it is moved forwards or backwards by means of a ratchet fitting over an adjusting nut. Others are hydraulically moved or have grease pumped into them. They all, however, are mounted on an eccentric axle arm. When this has been adjusted to its fullest extent then a link must be removed from the track. Crown copyright.

1 Guide roller
2 Lubricating nipple
3 Rebound bracket
4 Axle arm
5 Filler plug
6 Locking plate
7 Hub nut
8 Lubricating nipple
9 Hub cap
10 Axle arm
11 Bumper

This is a good view, again showing the suspension units. Here can be seen to good advantage the massive springs inside the units, and the rebound pads fitted in case of the axle arm being compressed beyond its limits. This prevents metal to metal wear on the unit. Crown copyright.

Although in very poor condition this shows the layout of the bins on either side of the hull. Towards the rear can be seen the fuel filler and the exhaust pipe

Shot from above showing the armoured cap over the fuel filler and the exhaust outlet. To make sure that the wrong fuel was not used the word PETROL was embossed on the casting of the lid. Author.

Rear view showing the fire extinguisher mounted on the rear of the bins. These types of extinguishers were made of brass and today are selling for at least £20. Author.

handset, reach in and press a button, which would sound a bleep in the commander's headset. Thus alerted, he could then select the relevant position on his controls and talk with the person outside.

This was an admirable idea with one major failing – human nature being what it is, the person who was outside using the phone would usually try to seek cover by sheltering behind the tracks! Not a recommended place to hide, as inevitably the tank would set off in reverse thus managing to age rather rapidly one frightened infantryman. I have actually seen an infantryman run away when the tank started

A view showing the headlight arrangement and sidelights just visible on the extreme edges of each wing. This is the very first Mk II Conqueror and can be seen from the road outside Stanley Barracks, Bovington, opposite the Tank Museum. Author.

Bovington's Mk I Conqueror at the rear showing the Infantry tank telephone box with stowage for the first-aid box above it. Author.

equipment and several people can testify to that by having been to close to it when it has been unclamped and the crew have kicked it down to lie flush with the rear hull. It is of interest that the early prototypes of Chieftain were fitted with Conqueror-style gun crutches.

ARMOUR

We have already seen that the two main requirements for Conqueror were the ability to destroy enemy armour at long range, and also to be able to survive any return fire. To that end, Conqueror was for its day very well protected, both in design and amount of armour allocated to it. This is always the dilemma that designers face in how much in percentage terms can be allocated to protection, firepower and mobility. One feature of Conqueror's design that helped in protection was the shape of the turret. Its frontal width was vastly reduced from that of Centurion, only to be spoilt by quite a large shot trap caused by the large turret overhang at the rear. However, if the commander is doing his job right the enemy should not have the chance to engage the tank from the rear.

The armour thickness for the first batch was 3.5in (89mm) turret front and sides; 2.75in (70mm) on

to move in reverse, but for some reason he would not let go of the handset. The lead will stretch to about 10m, so we have this scene of an infantryman running for all he is worth attached to 56 tons of ferocious (in this case Chieftain) tank by means of the handset lead (I can say he lived to fight another day).

Fitted to the right-hand side of the rear plate was the gun crutch, which was used to secure the barrel when the tank was on rail or road transporters, or if the power control kit had broken down. For shipping, however, there was provision for moving the crutch so that the overhang was on the centre line of the vehicle as opposed to being over the right rear, making it easier to fit into the ship's holds. The crutch itself was a very solidly made item of

The aptly named vehicle 'William' showing the massive gun crutch on the right rear of the vehicle. This was used if the power gun kit broke down or to reduce vehicle length on road moves or when being transported. Author.

'Cognac' of the 5th Inniskilling Dragoon Guards showing the location of the twin sets of bazooka plates cable drum on the left rear of the turret and the gun fitted into the gun crutch. Private collection.

the rear of the turret, the large access plate on top of the turret was 1.25in (31mm) and the remainder of the turret roof was 2in (51mm).

The hull had a glacis plate of 5.12in (130mm) and the toe plate was 3in (76mm). The driver had 1.75in (44mm) for his overhead cover, the hull floor was given a maximum of .787in (20mm) and the vertical rear hull was 1.5in (38mm). On top of this were the bazooka plates or side skirts. Conqueror was unique as far as British tanks were concerned in that instead of having just one set of plates per side, it had two sets, with one set being fitted directly to the catwalks whilst the remainder were bolted to brackets fitted to the hull side. It was hoped that these would provide some measure of spaced armour. This all sounds very lavish and hopefully would have done the job. Thankfully the threat

never materialized and the only proof that the armour thickness would have kept out a 122mm armour-piercing round from the gun of the JS3 was on paper, the result of mathematical calculations and various firing trials.

To provide an example of how the gun/armour race had progressed, when the 4th/7th Royal Dragoon Guards were on the NATO tank ranges at Hohne they were on the first range period since converting back to the armoured Regiment role from armoured recce in Northern Ireland, A squadron was provided with a mint condition Conqueror that had never been fired at. It was duly towed down range after the squadron had clambered all over it and the older members of the squadron were regaling all with the inevitable 'when I was on Conquerors', type of stories. The

41 BA 56, in the late '70s before being taken down range and used as a hard target by A Squadron 4th/7th Royal Dragoon Guards on Hohne ranges. The inner set of bazooka plates shows up well in this shot. The two crewmen on the turret can give a measure of the size of Conqueror. Author.

first troop were then allowed to fire at it, and it must be borne in mind that this was only with Chieftain 120mm APDS practice which has a mild steel core instead of the tungsten steel of service ammunition. Several good hits were seen to be registered, including one spectacular one which launched the commander's hatch from the FCT into space for some considerable distance. Guns were then cleared and we all boarded a Stalwart and proceeded down range to examine the handiwork of 2nd troop.

What awaited us came as rather shock, as although only practice ammo had been used there were several good penetrations of the armour, although none had penetrated from a direct hit on the frontal armour. One shot in particular was impressive, as it had entered the front right

suspension unit and had then been deflected into the hull. It then travelled through the hull, angling upwards all the time until it exited near the top of the hull on the left-hand side, where it presumably carried on travelling for some distance. The most obvious comment was that if practice ammunition could do that then what on earth would the result be if service APDS were fired at it. However, that question was never answered because the firing of service APDS is very limited due to cost and safety, as the ricochet area of service ammo is tremendous.

However, some of that Squadron would soon find out the effect of APDS when they made their first visit to BATUS in Canada where they would be allowed ten rounds of APDS to fire at hard targets on a specially set-up range. In the early days of

This gives a good impression of the size of Conqueror compared to the soldiers alongside it. Note also the sheer size of the 120mm gun and the fume extractor halfway along the barrel. Interesting to note are the way that the engine decks are leaning back in the fully open position to allow the crews access to the engine compartment. Private collection.

BATUS a large amount of hard targets were in fact ex-Canadian Army Centurions. The experience of firing service ammunition and seeing the effects on the targets really has to be seen to understand it.

Apart from the small differences that we have seen,

the Conqueror Mk I and II were identical, with perhaps the best vehicles being the seven Caernarvons that were rebuilt to Conqueror standards. Throughout its brief life FV214 never altered in style or design and was never seriously upgraded.

5 Firepower

We saw in earlier chapters that the designers for the FV200 series which led to Conqueror had an uphill struggle to get their design into service due to the requirement for a universal tank. It is not always appreciated that however good an idea may be it is governed by an almost inescapable formula that cannot be deviated from in the design of Armoured Fighting Vehicles. These can be divided into three main headings, which are defined as firepower, mobility and protection. These criteria can be interpreted in any combination: the UK has always gone for firepower, protection and mobility. For example, with vehicles such as Centurion and Chieftain, both had good armour and lethal guns, but the mobility was not as good. Other countries such as Germany always favoured firepower and mobility above protection, such as the Leopard I and II. Conqueror was designed within the firepower, protection and mobility framework, for as we have seen the requirement was not for a new battle tank but a long-range specialized tank killer.

The requirement when specified was for a large calibre gun with sizes ranging through from 120mm–180mm (4.6–7in). This was felt to be the optimum calibre that would be needed not only to defeat the JS3, but also any future tanks that the Russians would be bound to produce. Any future tank was likely to be equipped with better armour and bigger guns. However, the problem with finding a gun with a large calibre and the long range that would be needed by any vehicle attempting to engage the JS3 was that at the time there was no such weapon in the British inventory. Although many guns were under trial, the gestation period before they actually came on line was going to be too long. In the end, a gun based on an American anti-aircraft weapon met the urgent need for a 120mm gun.

The design was taken and modified and put into production as the 120mm L1A1\2 ordnance quick

A slightly unusual shot showing a 120mm Conqueror barrel alongside a 20-pounder Centurion barrel with a lamp post alongside for comparison. Author.

firing gun. The gun was equipped initially with two types of ammunition, HE and APDS; HESH was issued later on. All types were of the split-ammunition variety, that is, the brass case containing the propellant charge and the projectile were separate for the first time in a British tank.

Provision was made for the stowage of thirty-five main armament rounds. As the spent cases would be very large and heavy it was felt that there must be a system that would automatically eject the cases from the turret, rather than have the loader throw them manually from the turret. This led to the installation of the Mollins ejector gear, which, as we have seen, was less than successful. It was, however, a first for a British tank, although it was known that the Russians were going to provide something on the next generation of Soviet tanks.

However, before we get the idea that the Mollins company was not very successful we must look at another idea to aid the loader. It had been felt that the loader would be very easily exhausted by the work of loading the cases, so an assisted rammer system was designed. The contract for designing and building this was awarded to Mollins on 24 November 1952. When the decision not to use the assisted ramming gear was taken, DRAC made the following remarks about the equipment: 'this is an excellent piece of equipment and all credit to the designers and the company in producing it.' This was praise indeed and one feels that the company would like to be remembered for that and not the ejection gear.

The main reason for not using the equipment was that although it was an excellent piece of engineering a loader could complete a full cycle of loading using HESH in 6.5 seconds, which was approximately 1 second quicker than the mechanical assistance. This has a parallel today where a loader with the Royal Scots Dragoon Guards actually beat the automatic loader of the French tank Lecrec. However, the automatic rammer would not go away and years later the trials crews for Chieftain found that they too were being given a rammer to aid loading. Unfortunately, it was found to be of no use so it was removed, and one

day a visiting VIP spotted the forlorn remains of the rammer in a corner of the vehicle hanger and asked about it. On being told that it had been dumped he was less than amused and proceeded to explain how it had cost £100,000 to develop. However, it was never seen again, much to the relief of all those concerned.

The fire-control equipment that was provided for Conqueror was, for the day, extremely lavish. Prior to this, all that the commander had to help him find the range was estimating using a map or by eyesight, both of which were unreliable. He could also hope that someone had already fired at something in the area and had recorded the range, or if he wished to fire APDS he could fire a HESH\HE round at his estimated range and then correct his fire from that. This was a very wasteful and none too tactical way of finding out the range, so the advent of a vehicle-borne rangefinder seemed like the answer to a prayer.

THE FIRE-CONTROL TURRET

In our look at the firepower of the vehicle we shall start with the commander's fire-control turret (FCT). As, noted earlier, for the first time in the RAC the commander was isolated from the remainder of the turret crew, feelings about which were divided. The FCT itself was designed to be able to traverse the full 360 degrees under power, but no provision was provided for emergency traverse by hand, which was a shortcoming that was to remain throughout the tank's service life. However isolated the commander may have been, many Conqueror commanders have said that if nothing else the location of the FCT and its height above the ground gave them a more than normal feeling of power. One can easily imagine that feeling as they drove through the German towns, with an indescrible noise from the steel-tyred wheels on steel tracks and the roaring of the exhaust.

The FCT was equipped with a 4ft 1in (125cm) base rangefinder, which gave the commander the facility to find the range from 400 out to 5,000yd

A good close up of the FCT showing the .30 Browning machine gun and its associated ammunition box. Also clearly seen are the commander's hatch locked in the open position, the cover for the left-hand eyepiece of the rangefinder and the sight head of the various optics within the FCT. Author.

(366–4,572m). The rangefinder was fitted right across the forward part of the FCT with the heads protected by movable armoured flaps controlled from within the FCT by cables on later vehicles, and by the commander manually opening them on earlier vehicles. It was of the coincidence type with a magnification of x10 and a field of view of 3 degrees. It was provided with electrical illumination of the internal adjuster and range scales. The controls of the rangefinder were fairly simple and consisted of the coincidence adjusting head which was a milled knob situated to the left of the eyepiece on the underside of the body. The infinity scale was illuminated by a dimmer switch on the commander's control box. The range scale was the most important part and was marked from 400–5,000 yd and could be viewed to the left of the

field of view in the rangefinder eyepiece. A focusing knob was also provided.

To find the range to a target the commander would lay the dividing line that was visible in his eyepiece on to the centre of the target, then he would adjust the rangefinder until the images above and below the line were in perfect coincidence. The range could then be read off from the left in his field of view, the whole operation being very much like the operation of a modern SLR camera.

A no. 8 telescopic sight was provided for use as the commander's main sight. This had a x6 optical system and a range scale. The sight consisted of three main parts – a collimator and linkage, reflector and linkage and a x6 telescope. The collimator was a housing that pivoted on an axis parallel to the main gun trunnions. The housing and

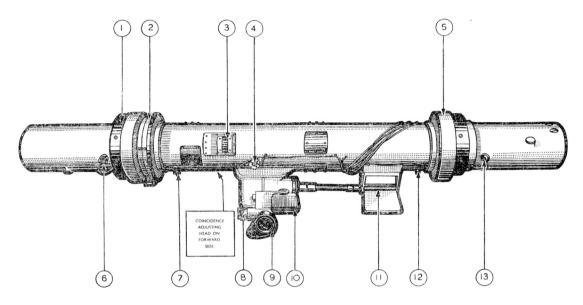

COINCIDENCE
ADJUSTING
HEAD ON
FORWARD
SIDE

1. Bearing locating ring
2. Elevation quadrants
3. Halving adjustment head
4. Range scale lamp housing
5. Bearing
6. Internal adjuster lamp housing
7. Desiccator union

8. Focusing screw
9. Eyepiece
10. Browpad
11. Working head
12. Desiccator union
13. Internal adjuster lamp housing

Gunnery book drawing of the rangefinder from the FCT showing the size and relative simplicity of the equipment.

the gunner's sight were linked together so that any movement of the gunner's sight rotated the collimator about its axis. Inside the collimator was a graticule similar to the one in the gunner's sight, so that when the FCT and main turret were lined up the commander could see exactly what the gunner had lain onto. The collimator was also provided with internal illumination.

The reflector was mounted along with the telescope in a sight mounting no. 7, which was secured to the roof of the FCT. There were two windows provided in the body of the reflector and the upper one protruded through the FCT roof to view the landscape. The lower window viewed the graticule when both turrets were in the line-up position. Another window at the bottom of the

reflector was situated directly above the object lens of the telescope. Within the reflector body two mirrors were connected by linkage to the rangefinder so that when the commander rotated the elevating handle the upper mirror raised or lowered the commander's field of vision. Moving simultaneously the lower mirror superimposed the collimator graticule onto the commander's field of view when the turrets were in the line-up position. This indicated the gunner's lay or, if the commander had overriding control, enabled him to lay the gun accurately.

The telescope was a x6 optical instrument that contained a range scale and was mounted with the reflector within the sight mounting no. 7 secured to the roof of the FCT. The sight was focused by

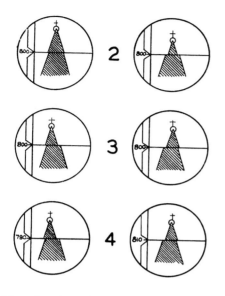

1. Halving and coincidence correct. Range scale reading true range of target—800 yds.

2. Halving head rotated causing vertical displacement of upper image

3. Halving correct. Coincidence adjustment head rotated causing lateral displacement of upper image ie, lack of coincidence

4. Halving and coincidence adjustment correct. Working head rotated causing lateral displacement of upper image and change of range scale reading.

More shots from the Conqueror gunnery pamphlet showing how the rangefinder was used and what the view would have been like for the commander. As mentioned in the text, the system is not unlike the focusing for an SLR camera. Crown copyright.

means of a knob on the left side of its body. The right-hand eyepiece contained a heater and the range scale was viewed through the left eyepiece. The scales were marked in the same way as those of the gunner's sight.

One final component made up this unit, and that was the range adjustment unit. This was situated below the FCT traverse controller; it was connected electrically with the range-scale driving motors. This enabled the commander to apply range on the no. 8 sight range scale and the gunner's range scale providing that the gun control equipment was running.

Range was applied to the scale by means of the range-adjustment unit, with the gun control equipment running, and any alteration made to the telescope range scale was also automatically

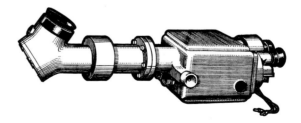

This shows the reflector, which with the telescope makes up the no. 8 sight in the FCT. Crown copyright.

The telescope no. 8. Looking through this the commander would have seen the same picture as the gunner when the FCT and main turret were lined up. Crown copyright.

applied to the gunner's range scale. Similarly, any alteration of the gunner's range scale would change the commander's scale and the tangent elevation of the gun.

The commander also had a periscopic sight no. 6 which was used to sight the commander's .30 Browning machine gun mounted on the left side of the FCT. The unit was linked to the gun and it contained a daylight-illuminated graticule for aiming. A tinted glass filter was provided for use to enable the graticule to be seen against a bright background. The sight was linked to the machine gun so that line of sight followed it; this allowed the weapon to be fired from under cover.

The commander also had two no. 7 periscopes fitted in the FCT. These were fitted one either side of the no. 6 periscope sight. Each sight comprised two prisms fitted into a metal case. It was possible to adjust the field of view of each sight by turning a collimator screw in the centre. The screw worked in conjunction with a spring plate fitted inside the sight body. If the object prism became damaged it would be replaced from a spare carried on the vehicle. The part of the sight inside the FCT was fitted with a blackout shutter, to be used when the interior lights were in use. Use of the blackout shutter, though, meant that the observation available to the commander was severely limited. The sights gave a field of view of 42 degrees looking down with 10 degrees looking up. To obtain 360 degrees of vision whilst closed down the FCT was traversed through its full 360 degrees.

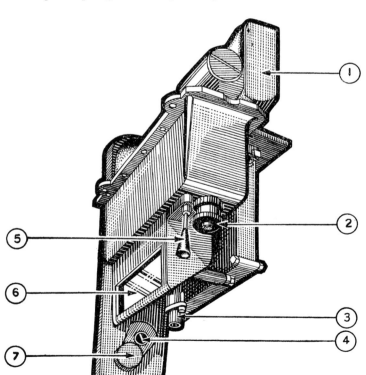

1. Upper prism assembly

2. Lateral adjustment knob

3. Connection for wiper drive

4. Spindle

5. Filter operating knob

6. Lower prism assembly

7. Vertical adjustment knob

This shows the sight no. 6 that was used by the commander to sight the commander's machine gun; this enabled him to use the weapon from under armour cover if he needed to. Crown copyright.

THE GUNNER'S CONTROLS

Although all this gave the commander the facility to range, apply range and correct the lay, he could only do this by power; fine laying of the gun had to be done by the gunner. Sighting, laying, observing and making and applying corrections were all part of the gunner's job and the commander should really be worrying about commanding the vehicle and letting the gunner get on with the shoot.

To aid him in this, the gunner was provided with various instruments and controls. The most important of these was his sight periscopic no. 10 Mk I. This was equipped with two levels of magnification – x1 for general viewing and scanning, and also in the x1 window was an engraved circle representing the field of view of the x6 eyepiece. Below the x1 window was the x6 eyepiece, which contained a graticule pattern with a central aiming mark. The design of the graticule allowed the gunner to calculate aim off in mils. The unit of measure of mils was chosen to replace degrees and minutes as it allowed for much greater accuracy, there being 6,400 mils to a circle compared to 360 degrees, so a much finer calculation could be given. The lenses of the sight were bloomed to improve performance. This led to the slightly rosy/pink colour that could be seen in optics. The graticule of the x6 could be illuminated by means of a 3v-pea type bulb and the degree of brightness could be controlled from a dimmer switch on the gunner's control box.

The sight head was protected by an external flap, which could be lowered when the sight was not in use, and a washer and wiper system was also provided to aid the removal of dirt and mud. The sight was mounted in mounting sight AFV no. 5 Mk I; this supported the sight and also included the range gear, which consisted of six main components:

The Elevation Bracket

The elevation bracket was pivoted from the turret roof and was connected to the mounting through a rod to the false trunnion. The lower end of the bracket was connected to the sight gear by a rack,

The sight no. 10 Mk I, the gunner's sight. Of note is the single rubber eyepiece with to its left one of the adjusters for the graticule pattern. Forward of the sight can be seen the 4-pin power plug which would marry up with the male socket once the sight was mounted. Crown copyright.

which engaged with the range adjuster. A toothed arc on the elevation bracket was engaged with the range drum-driving pinion in the sight gear bracket.

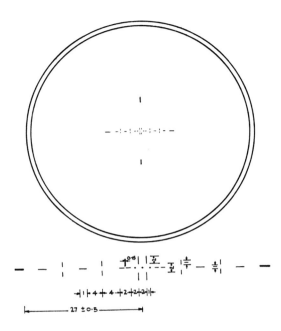

The graticule pattern as seen in the gunner's sight. As can be seen, it is a very simple pattern. The vertical and horizontal lines would have been used in the procedures for tracking a moving target. Crown copyright.

The Sight Gear Bracket

This was fitted to the left side of the periscope mounting and connected to the elevation bracket, so that any rotation of range adjuster moved the sight bracket and periscope mounting, thus putting on or taking off range. Provision was made for the fitting of a clinometer no. 2 Mk I, which was to be fitted at a later date. Once it had been fitted it meant that the vehicle could carry out full indirect firing.

The Range Scale

The range scale was mounted on the sight gear bracket and contained all the range scales, which were visible to the gunner by means of a range-scale reflector situated on the left of his sight. The scales were marked for APC, HEAT, HVAP, APDS and MG with HESH coming later. The APC, HVAP and APDS scales were marked from 0–300yd

(0–274m) at intervals of 200yd (183m) and were numbered every 400yd (366m). The HEAT scale was marked and numbered from 0–3,000yd (0–2,743m) at a spacing of 200yd (183m). The HE scale was marked from 0–3,000yd at intervals of 100yd (91m) and numbered every 200yd. The scale that was used for the machine gun had what was known as a battle mark that represented 400yd and this appeared between the 1,400 (1,280m), and 1,600 (1,463m) ranges on the APDS scale. The use of a battle mark was to simplify laying on of the weapon, so that within a set distance the gunner would just lay the battle mark onto the target instead of having to try to find the range on the scale. This would be important if infantry were approaching the tank at close range.

The Cursor

This was also fitted to the sight bracket and allowed the accurate setting of the range marking by placing the required range under the engraved cursor line – simple but effective. A lamp was also fitted to enable the cursor line and range scales to be viewed in all lighting conditions.

Magslip Resetter Unit

When all the gun control equipment was running, any movement of the range-scale adjuster caused the gun to be moved in the same direction and by the required amount of movement to alter the tangent elevation of the gun. This was done by linking the sight bracket to the magslip unit by means of steel tape, so that any movement of the sight bracket immediately rotated the magslip unit drive, causing a signal to be fed to an amplifier which caused the gun to be moved in the required direction and amount.

Trunnion Tilt Indicator

This operated very much in the manner of an ordinary spirit level in that a vial containing fluid and a bubble was set parallel to the gun trunnions

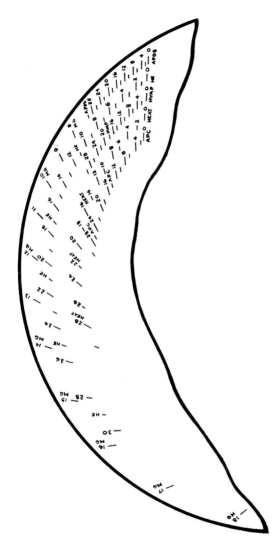

This is the range scale as would be visible to the gunner; a similar one was also seen by the commander. On the scale can be seen markings for ammunition that Conqueror was never destined to fire such as HEAT and HVAP. Also marked on the scale are the ranges for use with the machine gun. Crown copyright.

on the face of the magslip unit. Inscribed above it was a set of scales, and by use of these the gunner would apply aim-off to the gun to compensate for the cant of the gun.

To enable the gunner to apply and measure line

correction and switches he was equipped with a traverse indicator. The face of this was split into two scales, both being coloured, red for the right, and green for left. The inner scale was marked in 100s of mils and the outer in units of mils; the instrument was internally illuminated. It received its information from a transmitter unit situated on the left-hand side of the turret and in mesh with the turret race.

The gunner had control of the power elevation and traverse controls for the gun, and also provided were a handle (early models) or handwheel (late models) which drove a hydraulic pump to give hand elevation. A two-speed hand traverse handle was also provided, which could be used by the gunner either to make a fine lay or in emergencies or servicing to traverse the turret. There was also a facility for emergency power control for traverse only.

Using these controls, full rotation of the turret could be achieved in 24 seconds for power traverse;

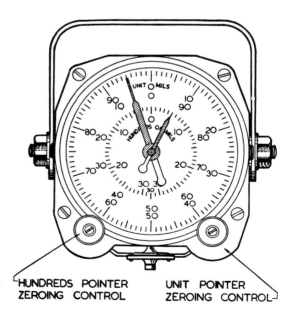

HUNDREDS POINTER
ZEROING CONTROL

UNIT POINTER
ZEROING CONTROL

The traverse indicator, which is mounted in front of the gunner, was used to show how many degrees left or right the turret had been traversed. It could also be used to set up for fixed line firing. Crown copyright.

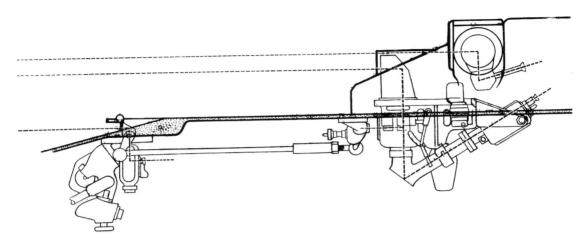

A very good see-through view of all the fire-control equipment showing how each piece linked in with the next to produce, for the time, a very effective fire-control system. Crown copyright.

emergency power traverse was achieved in one rotation in 145 seconds. The FCT had a rotation speed of one revolution in 10 seconds. The gunner also had controls to govern the use of the sight washer's wipers, the armoured cover for his sight and the selector for main or co-ax armament. To fire the weapons electrically he had a firing switch on his power elevation controller and for mechanical firing of both weapons he was equipped with two foot pedals. The commander could also fire electrically both weapons from his FCT.

The gun control equipment was an electrically operated system drawing power from the batteries and the aux. gen. The main components of the system comprised a traverse gearbox, which was secured to the main turret forward of the gunner's seat and it meshed in with the rack fitted to the hull. When power was applied to the electric motor motion was transmitted to the rack and the turret would traverse; this also applied to hand and emergency traverse. (Should the gun strike a solid object the gears are protected from possible damage by the inclusion of a spring-loaded slipping clutch within the gear train.) The gearbox had its own oil pump to circulate oil to lubricate the gears and bearings. The hand traverse unit was a two-part

component, the handle assembly was bolted to a bracket on the main gearbox and connected by means of a shaft and ball joint to the worm drive and dog clutch assembly in the top part of the main gearbox. When power traverse was employed the dog clutch was automatically disengaged, preventing the hand traverse handle from rotating and injuring the gunner.

The elevation gearbox was fitted to the right side of the semi-automatic bracket in trunnions, which allowed rotary movement when the gun was elevated or depressed. Pivoted from the turret roof was the elevation rack, which was engaged with a rack pinion in the gearbox. The gears were powered by a permanently coupled electric motor and like the traverse box they were protected from possible damage from barrel strikes by the inclusion of a friction clutch within the system. The hand elevation gear was a hydraulic pump driven by a handwheel and connected by means of flexible tubing to a hydraulic motor on the main gearbox. This was in turn connected to a dog clutch on the main shaft of the gearbox. When power elevation was in use the dog clutch was disengaged again to prevent injury to the gunner by its rotating. Elevation and depression, stops were fitted to limit the elevation to 15 degrees or 270 mils and 7 degrees or 126 mils depression, apart from when the gun was over the back decks. As the gun approached a stop, cam-operated switches reduced the power to the motor to prevent damage to the equipment.

THE CONQUEROR'S WEAPONRY

Having looked at the controls that were available to the commander and gunner let us now take a look at the weapons that were available to them. The main reason for Conqueror's existence was to bring to the battlefield the 120mm gun, which as we have already seen was based on an American design from an anti-aircraft weapon. The same gun was fitted to the American M103, which was the American attempt to get the 120mm into service. It suffered a lot of problems and in the end it was taken on by the United States Marines in its M103A1 version as heavy support for beach landings, the American Army having given up on it. The same weapon was also fitted to the British Conway. The Conway was known as the 120mm Centurion, and was at one time going to be built in very large numbers. It was conceived as a way of getting the 120mm into the regiments that would be quicker than waiting for Conqueror to be developed and then produced. The weapon was carried on a Centurion hull with a large, thinly armoured turret, but in the end only one was built and this can be seen today at the Tank Museum at Bovington. The gun itself was 24ft 5in (7.4m) long and weighed 6,578lb (2,984kg), and a fume extractor was fitted halfway down the barrel.

The ordnance quick-firing 120mm tank L1A1 or L1A2 gun, to give it its full War office specification, was a 120mm nominal and 4.7in actual calibre weapon weighing 2 tons 18cwt 2qtr or 6,578lb with a length of 294.35ins. It was fitted with a horizontal sliding block-type breech with a semi-automatic action. This meant that the loader would manually open the breech for the first round but subsequently the breech would open automatically, leaving the loader to close it by hand once a round had been loaded. To control the recoil of the gun it was fitted into a mounting, .30 gun no. 1 Mk I. This mounting also held the recoil system which consisted of three cylinders, of which two were oil-filled buffers to absorb the recoil energy and the third was air-charged to return the gun to the run-out position ready to fire again. Two types of firing gear were fitted, one electrically finger-operated and the other mechanically foot-operated. The barrel was a single forging with interrupted threads at one end for attachment of the breech ring; midway along the barrel was a machined surface and external threads for the fitting of the fume extractor. Early versions did not have a fume extractor and a sheet metal cover was fitted in lieu. The L1A1 differed from the L1A2 by having a thread at the muzzle end.

The mounting consisted of a cradle, which was the part which projected through the front of the turret and supported the mantlet as well as the gun. On either side of the rear of the cradle a housing was formed to receive the left and right buffers. Situated on the left side was a cradle for the machine gun. The mantlet, which formed part of the nose of the turret, was made from a steel armour casting. It was fitted to the forward edge of the

Showing the cradle that the 120mm gun would have been mounted in. The large central hole is for the barrel while the smaller holes either side are for the recoil buffers that control the gun on firing. The large object on the left lower side is the recuperator, which would have returned the gun to the firing position. Author.

View through the top of the turret with the access plate removed showing clearly on the right hand side the dummy trunnion and linkage. Author.

A different view of the same vehicle, 41 BA 92, on Salisbury Plain showing the very large breech block with the breech in the closed position. Just visible on the front left wall are the stowage racks for the projectiles. Author.

cradle, and there was also a hole in the mantlet for the machine gun. The fitting of a canvas dust cover closed off the gap between the turret forward edge and the mantlet rear edge.

Part of the weapon system was the Mollins ejector gear, of which we have heard so much. This consisted of three major components. A base unit was situated on the turret turntable to the rear of the main armament. The top half was curved to form a chute, which was intended to direct a spent case to an exit door in the turret wall. To drive this, a motor and transmission were fitted and when the system was activated the motor would drive a chin mechanism which would lift the case from the base unit up forward of the FCT and open the door and eject the case. Once the case had been ejected the system reversed itself ready to start again. A control box was fitted which contained an isolating switch and a timing switch. In dire emergency the system could be operated by hand.

The operation of the 120mm was basically that the gun would be loaded by hand using the two-part split ammunition with the case being percussion ignited. When the gun was fired the gun would recoil but under control of the twin buffers. Once this had taken place the gun would then be returned to the firing position by the pneumatic recuperator, during this run-out period the breech would open

automatically and the empty case would be ejected automatically and land on the ejection gear ready to be removed from the turret.

The ammunition that was available was of the split nature, that is, projectile and case were loaded as separate items. Natures used were APDS, DS PRAC, HE, with HESH later replacing the HE round. No smoke or canister ammunition was provided – as it was not thought necessary as Conqueror was not a battle tank it and so needed as many tank killing rounds as possible.

Performance figures for the main natures carried were that APDS would penetrate 446mm (17.3 in) at 1,000yd (914m) and had a muzzle velocity of 4,700ft/sec (1,433m). HESH would penetrate 120mm (4.6in) at 1,000yd with a muzzle velocity of 2,500 ft/sec (762m). No figures are given for the performance of HE; as already stated it had been superseded by 1960.

The decision to use split ammo was taken for many reasons, but one of the main ones was that a 120mm fixed round would have been too heavy and unwieldy for the loader to manage on his own. The idea of automatic loaders and ejection systems had been suggested, and in fact a system where the gun was returned to set limits and then the case ejected had been mocked up and proved, but in the end the Mollins gear was chosen. One aspect of the size and weight of the ammunition became apparent from the troop trials carried out in BAOR to test the rates of fire achieved by the loader. Compared to the requirements laid down by BAOR and those of the War Office, it was felt that a loader could achieve the rates of fire required by BAOR, but possibly not those of the War Office. These requirements were for a sustained rate of fire from the main armament of twenty rounds in 30 minutes and a complete stowage of the full load of thirty-five rounds in 55 minutes. Also, the War Office called for an initial rate of fire of four rounds in the first minute followed by three rounds per minute for the next four minutes, giving a total of sixteen rounds. To test out these figures, a trial was held at the Gunnery School, RAC Centre, and the results showed that the requirements for BAOR could be met, but not those of the War Office. Loaders were picked for their physique, or the PT staff ran special body-

training classes for Conqueror loaders. This was not really satisfactory, as there needed to be interchangeability between crew members and not everyone could be muscle-bound.

The FV214 also carried two .30 machine guns. One was fitted to the left side of the FCT and the other co-axially with the main armament. The loader was responsible for the maintenance of the co-axial mounted gun during firing periods. He had to ensure that the ammunition was fed to the weapon and would not get trapped and cause a stoppage, and if a stoppage did occur he would clear it (unless the tank was on the move). The Browning had a rate of fire of 425–450 rounds a minute and could be shot out to a range of 1,800yd (1,646m) depending on visibility or the range at which the tracer round burnt out. Originally, the Conqueror was to be equipped with one of two new British tank machine guns that were to have been built after

The .30 Browning machine gun mounted on the FCT. The angle iron bracket is not part of the vehicle but has been added by the Tank Museum. Author.

a competition to see which was best. In the end neither weapon was taken into service and the .30 Browning soldiered on until its replacement as an AFV weapon by the 7.62 GPMG. Those who have experienced both guns would go for the Browning every time – although you had to nurse it along it was a more reliable gun and easier to clean than the 7.62 GPMG (plus the ammunition belts being made of fabric were extremely useful for securing kit to the vehicle). The commander was also equipped with the Browning on his FCT. A total of thirty boxes of Browning ammunition were carried, with most in the turret and some in the FCT.

The main mode of operation to control all of this enormous amount of equipment was to be in the power mode, although for very fine laying the hand controls would be used. Whilst the power system was all right for laying the weapon, the biggest omission was the decision not to include a full stabilization system. This was mainly due to a General Staff decision that in view of the role that Conqueror was to play on the battlefield full stabilization would be an expensive luxury. This was probably a fair statement in the eyes of the General Staff, but it made hard work for the vehicle crews left to fend with second best again.

The system that was eventually employed allowed normal power control of the equipment whilst static, but as soon as the vehicle moved off with all of the gun control equipment running, a centrifugal switch driven from the vehicle speedo was activated. Once a speed of more than 2mph had been reached the gun would automatically be placed under gyro unit control; this maintained the gun between the limits of +1 to 15 degrees. The only control that the gunner had over this was a trim controller, but this only allowed him to make alterations within the limits already mentioned. This effectively ruled out being able to engage targets on the move. The vehicle also had to be allowed to come to a standstill and a pause of 3 seconds had to elapse before the gunner had control of the gun kit again. Thus having taken your tank across country and finally got your vehicle into an excellent fire position you would be sat there with

your long gun barrel waving aimlessly about in the air, much to the amusement of the Centurion crews.

Of course, although Conqueror had its bad points, there were good points as well. There is no doubt in my mind that Conqueror could perform the task it was set, and that was to kill JS3. With an APDS penetration of 446mm (17.4in) against the intelligence estimate of the JS3's 200mm (7.8in) frontal turret armours (although it was later accepted that the armour on JS3 was in fact a 200mm basis, that is, the combination of the thickness and the sloping of the armour), the effects would have been devastating. Conqueror, in its turn, was proof against the Soviet vehicle's gun, except for certain small areas of the nose plate, and no commander should be thinking of letting an enemy vehicle get a shot in that area anyway. It was also felt that in spite of projected Soviet improvements to their guns Conqueror would still provide a reasonable level of protection in its turret and glacis plate. Centurion crews that I have spoken to have always said that the feeling of the great big beast lurking a bound behind them in overwatches was always a reassuring thought.

The last weapons that were carried by Conqueror were twelve smoke dischargers fitted on either side of the turret, six each side. These were used to give local smoke and were fired by the commander from his station in the FCT. The smoke grenades carried were the no. 80 white phosphorous, which when coming into contact with the air would give an instantaneous smoke screen. Eighteen of these were carried; also twelve hand grenades and ninety-one magazines of 9mm (0.35in), each containing thirty-two rounds for the crew's personal weapons and twelve Very cartridges were also carried.

A TYPICAL ENGAGEMENT

Finally, let us look at how a typical engagement would take place. We can assume that the gun is already loaded with the correct nature of ammunition, so the commander and gunner are using their power controls to scan the ground in front of

Conqueror Mk II that has been used as a hard target on Otterburn ranges for many years. Although the HEAT rounds have destroyed most of the area around the driver's cab it has taken a long time, showing how well the armour did work. The white colour scheme was to enable blind anti-tank gunners to pick up the target! Courtesy Steve Osfield.

them. We will assume that the commander is the one to spot the target. He would then lay the centre line in the rangefinder on to the centre of the target, and then by rotating the upper head would bring the two images together. Once he has completed this he can read the range in his left eyepiece, and if he is satisfied that the range is correct he would set the range on to his and the gunner's range scales by means of the range setting unit. During this time, he would also be issuing his fire order which tells the gunner and the loader what type of engagement they are going to carry out, which would also give the gunner some idea of how far away the target is. During this, the commander would have pressed the line-up switch on top of his power control and the main turret would traverse on to the target with the FCT contra-rotating. The gun would assume the correct elevation by means of the magslip unit combined with the elevation supplied by the range setter unit.

Once the two turrets are lined up, the injected image from the gunner's sight is projected into the right eyepiece of the commander's sight by means of the collimator unit. Once the commander is happy, he can then give the order to fire and if all goes well that will be the end of yet another enemy

tank. This, of course, all happens rather quicker than can be appreciated from the written word, and if you were to watch an RAC turret crew in action all that you would be able to make out would be a blur of actions from the loader, plus a lot of seemingly incomprehensible shouting from the commander and gunner. If all does not go to plan and the first round misses the gunner would straight away go into a well-rehearsed routine of corrections; if necessary, the commander could override him and issue his own corrections. Or if the commander was happy with the way that the gunner was carrying out the corrections and drills,

Another comparison view of the 120mm alongside Centurion this time, though, a 105mm gun. Centurion is on the left of the picture. The shiny portion in the centre of the barrels is the machined area covered by the fume extractor. M. Hiscock.

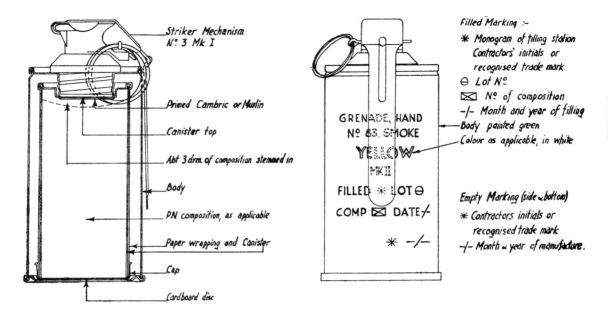

Striker Mechanism
Nº 3 Mk I

Primed Cambric or Muslin

Canister top

Abt 3 drm. of composition stemmed in

Body

PN composition, as applicable

Paper wrapping and Canister

Cap

Cardboard disc

GRENADE, HAND
Nº 83. SMOKE
YELLOW
MK II
FILLED ✳ LOT ⊖
COMP ⊠ DATE ⊣

✳ ⊣

Filled Marking :–

✳ Monogram of filling station
   Contractors' initials or
   recognised trade mark.
⊖ Lot Nº
⊠ Nº of composition
⊣ Month and year of filling
Body painted green
Colour as applicable, in white

Empty Marking (side ⊾ bottom)

✳ Contractors initials or
   recognised trade mark
⊣ Month ⊾ year of manufacture.

Handbook drawing of the no. 80 grenade as used in the smoke dischargers mounted either side of the turret. These were fitted into the discharger and then the safety pin removed. They were very dangerous being filled with white phosphorous. The advantage of using this is that as soon as it comes into contact with the atmosphere it starts to give out a smokescreen. This is something that a chemical-based compound does not do.

the commander could then traverse his FCT off the current target and look for another and when he has found one he can take the range to it ready for the whole sequence to start again. This system has been adopted in Challenger II and is called the Hunter – Killer mode. However, Challenger is doing it all by computers and electronics, although either way the empty case would have been ejected from the turret and the loader would be loading the next round ready to continue the engagement.

Whilst this is taking place the driver is not completely forgotten way down in the driver's cab. He would be keeping the engine running and also looking out for targets. Sometimes it is the driver who will pick up the target first. He has to be ready to engage reverse and move very quickly, as the tank that stays in the same position after firing several rounds is the tank that will be killed.

6 Variants

Although the FV214 was meant to be a one-off vehicle and employed in the long-range anti-tank role, a job that it was finally allowed to do after many fights for survival, work was carried out on the variants that had been planned for the universal tank from which the Conqueror owed its lineage.

For us to obtain an idea of the planned variants that were due to be based around the Conqueror hull we must first go back to the beginning of the universal tank programme and A45. This, as we have seen, was the infantry tank version of Centurion mounting the 17-pounder on the prototype, but it was designed to be able to mount the 20-pounder on the production models. In an attempt to accomodate a fifth crew member a remotely controlled machine gun was mounted over the left-hand over-trackguard. This was necessary, as it was a firm requirement of the A45 that a flame thrower supplied from a trailer be fitted. This meant the permanent installation of all the pipes required for the flame equipment, and also the need for the flame gun to be situated in the glacis plate with a co-driver. There were many variants proposed on the A45 chassis and from this sprang the requirement for the universal tank concept, which became the FV200 series. FV200 itself was never allocated to a particular vehicle but became the generic family title, much as FV7000 has become with the CVRT series of vehicles based on a common chassis.

FV201 was meant to be the universal or capital tank and considerable research and development had been carried out by the middle of 1948 when cancellation of the project was raised. It was finally cancelled in April 1949, but by then three prototypes had been built and would be used for FV214 development. The turret being designed for this vehicle was to have mounted a 20-pounder, a co-ax machine gun and a cross-turret rangefinder, but in the end it was never built. As an interim measure a Centurion II turret mounting a 17-pounder and a Centurion III turret with the 20-pounder were fitted, while the remaining vehicle had the Windsor ballast turret fitted. The design was intended to be able to mount either a flame thrower or a dozer blade with both able to be fitted in the field with REME support, and a requirement for conversion to the DD role was also stipulated. Mounted on the front left corner of the glacis plate was the intended location for the remotely controlled bow machine gun, protected by an armoured housing, much the same as had been fitted to A45.

The driver was to have been provided with three periscopes mounted in the hull, which would have given him excellent vision. As the tank had to be capable of being fitted with flame equipment, the pipes for this were to be installed during construction so that if a vehicle were to be converted to the flame role there would be no need to remove components to lay the pipes. This insistence on the pipework being built in was the result of DRAC emphatically refusing to allow flame fuel to be carried inside the vehicle; this was rather a wise decision on his part. The flame thrower equipment that may well have been placed into service was given the name of 'Red Cyclops', although this was never confirmed officially. It was designed from the outset to be fitted in the field with REME assistance. The tank was to pull a flame trailer weighing 13 tons (13,208 kg), which contained the flame fuel and the air bottles to propel the fuel; operating pressure was gauged at 800lb per sq. in and the trailer was equipped with the run-flat type of tyres. If fitted, the flame head was to be situated centrally on the lower glacis, which would require a 6in (152mm) hole. When not fitted, a plate of armour covered the hole. Traverse of the flame head was 120 degrees left and right with an elevation of +30/-5 degrees. It was controlled by the flame gunner with a set of controls not unlike a bike handlebars, and it was claimed that a range of 150yd (137m) could be achieved. FV201 was also designed to be fitted with a dozer blade if required and once again the fittings for carrying a dozer blade were put in place during production. Conversion was felt to be within the scope of an Armoured Workshop. If a close-support version of FV201 had been produced it was felt that the blade could be fitted during production. It was envisaged that Duplex Drive could also be fitted by the workshops. This was the invention of a man called Nicholas Strauser, and had been fitted to Shermans for D-Day. It basically consisted of a canvas screen supported around the tank and held upright by struts, which gave the tank the displacement needed to float. Propeller units were fitted and were driven from power take-off units driven from the final drive. All this gave a vehicle which weighed 55 tons (55,880kg) laden, a length of 25ft 6in (93m), a ground pressure of 9.84lb per sq. in, a crew of five with a top speed of 19mph (30km/h) and radius of 110 miles (177km). A Rolls Royce 800bhp Meteor fuel-injected engine was fitted, and a 20-pounder gun with stabilization was the main armament.

At a user meeting on 14–15 July 1947 the user was shown a mock of what FV210 was due to look like, and this mock-up was again converted to represent the vehicle as fitted with the DD equipment. This, however, was only carried out on one side of the vehicle, the left hand with the right remaining as a gun tank.

CONQUEROR'S PROTOTYPES

The prototypes of FV201 were put to various uses. The A41 soft boat prototype had been the original Centurion hull built by AEC, but by November 1946 it had been cut and a 15in (381mm) length inserted. This was so that it could be used to represent FV210. The main use that it was put to was in the development of the dozer blade that was envisaged to be fitted to the FV201. The original type of blade resembled that used during World War II, in that the arms coming from the blade were fitted to the side of the tank hull. However, it seems that by January 1953 a new type of blade was being tested, having hydraulic rams fitted to the hull on the glacis and connecting to the rear of the blade. Also at this stage it was still being discussed whether the FV214 would be fitted with the new blade. The new blade was eventually fitted to the soft boat hull and from December 1956 to November 1957 it was used for trial work against obstacles such as concrete emplacements, concrete obstacles, trees and so on that might be encountered on the battlefield. This sort of testing caused severe damage both to the blade and to the hull. However, after a full strip inspection the vehicle was actually pronounced fit to carry on, but there is no record of it ever being used again.

P1

This was built by English Electric in mild steel and was running with a Centurion III turret fitted by October 1947. After completing 300 miles (483km) running it was taken into workshops and completely stripped down and inspected. Once it had been rebuilt it was then moved to Chobham where it was fitted with Centurion-type pagoda louvres in a trial to improving the vehicle's cooling. In October 1948 it commenced mileage trials, which involved driving the vehicle around circuits in an attempt to obtain high mileage, so that various components could be observed. Once 1,000 miles (1,609km) had been completed it was weighted to simulate the all-up 60 tons (60,960kg) of the specialist FV200 vehicles. After 1,336 miles (2,150km) the Centurion II turret was removed and a stripped-out Centurion III turret fitted. By now, the vehicle was listed as a component tester as it did not resemble either FV221 or FV214. The 2,393 miles (3,850km) mark was achieved in March 1951, but by then it was suffering breakdowns of suspension, cooling, ignition final drives, brakes and gearbox. By July 1954 it had been used for mine trials and had suffered considerable damage, and after that there is no record of what happened to it.

P2

This was the flame prototype fitted with the Centurion III turret and 20-pounder. The flame equipment was ready by July 1948, and was being fitted by October 1949. By then, the decision not to fit flame equipment to FV214 had been taken, but the trials continued with the ultimate view of fitting the flame equipment into Centurion. The vehicle was running by April 1950, but the flame kit was immediately removed and the vehicle was provided with extra weights to simulate the expected all-up weight of FV214.

P3

This vehicle was intended to be completed by mid-1950 and it was planned to be the prototype of the DD tank, ready for trials with the LCT8 modified to take the FV200 series vehicles. The complete vehicle was ready and at the FVPE by October 1950, but had to wait till March 1951 for the modified landing craft to be ready. It would seem that this vehicle did actually manage to swim, although the sight of 60 tons of tank hanging from a flotation screen must surely defy the imagination and no doubt presented a most impressive sight. In March 1959 it was reported that the same flotation screen from P3 was being used in trials to develop a DD system for Centurion.

It had been proposed that there would be a requirement for two types of AVRE in the programme – one would be turreted and carry a large calibre demolition gun, whilst the other would be an assault bridge carrier.

FV202 AVRE (T)

This was to be the turreted version of the AVRE and would have a Centurion-type turret fitted with a 6.5 demolition gun, with plans to make this weapon a recoilless one. The fire-control system was to be similar to FV201 but without the stabilizer. It was also intended to be able to tow a 10-ton (10,160kg) AVRE trailer. The hull was of similar design to FV201 and was also proposed to be adapted to carry such engineer devices as mine rollers, mine-laying equipment and even to be able to tow an 80ft (24m) mobile bridge on its own independent tracked dolly trailer. The intention was to produce a prototype, but the project was cancelled in favour of FV215A in 1949.

FV203 AVRE (L)

This was to have carried the assault bridge and was to have been able to carry the same fittings as FV202; also it was to be able to tow an AVRE trailer based on the FV201 flame-thrower trailer. It was a high-sided vehicle similar in shape and layout to FV222, the ARV Mk II. The driver's seat and controls were raised and lowered as one complete station for head out and closed down driving. The vehicle was also expected to be fitted with or to have fitted a fascine cradle and mine-laying equipment. One prototype was built in mild steel, and although the project was cancelled in April 1949 in favour of FV215A, the prototype was running at FVRDE in October 1949, but by then was classed as a component tester only. It had completed 2,500 miles (4,023km) by April 1950 and probably finished its days as a mobile test rig being driven over live mines in aid of research into

Prototype for the FV 200 series ARV/AVRE. This was to be the AVRE version without the 165mm demolition gun in a Centurion turret. Tank Museum.

mine-proof tracks during August 1960. The mock-up had been built in 1-in steel plate instead of the usual plywood used for mock-ups. One can only assume that this was so that the various engineers fittings could be welded on to the hull and have some strength. It was converted to a full-length mock-up of the Ark-launched ramp mechanism. The Ark was a method of bridging a gap greater than could be achieved by using a conventional bridge layer. The Ark had a series of ramps at either end, drove into the gap and unfolded the ramps, thus creating a bridge for vehicles to cross.

due to power take-off and transmission problems. It was suggested that a separate flail power unit be provided with a view to using a 1,000bhp engine. The concept as originally designed had only called for the detonation of a mine fuse, but by using a 1000hp engine the requirement was changed to total detonation of the mine. However, in doing this a new vehicle would almost certainly be required which was very much against the requirement for a flail tank. This conflict was so great that the project continued for the majority of the time at a very low priority until disappearing from sight altogether.

FV204

The universal flail was designed to be carried by a normal FV201 gun tank, but this proved impractical

FV205

This was a proposal for medium anti-tank weapon carrier. However, by July 1948 a decision had still

Flail Tanks

It had long been recognized that for any invasion of Europe one of the threats that Allied armour would have to face would be the threat of massed minefields. The traditional way of clearing these was by hand, both slow and very dangerous.

It was decided that a mechanical means was needed and the answer was found in the flail tank. Some flail tanks were conversions of hulls fitted with the flails but no offensive armament; others could still utilize their main armament.

In its simplest form the flail tank had a pair of arms that projected forward off the vehicle. Fitted to these arms was a large power-driven drum. The power for this could come from a power take-off unit from the engine or another engine could be fitted, especially to drive the drum. Fitted to the drum were chains that carried a large weight on the end of them. In use, the flail tank would move up to the start of the minefield, the drum would then be started and once the chains were flailing the ground the tanks would move forward.

The theory was that the weight and force of the blow would detonate any anti-tank mines in the path of the vehicle whilst only damaging the chain that struck it. The flail tank driving over them would deal with anti-personnel mines, as the charge contained in them would not damage the tank. This all had to be conducted at a very slow speed, 1–3mph, thus making the flail an easy target; however, the system did work and would clear a lane that was a tank-width wide. If a wider lane was required then the flails would work in echelon, thus creating a wide lane.

Even today, any soldiers covering a minefield are taught to engage any vehicle that is seen to be carrying mine-clearing equipment, be it flail, roller or plough-equipped. In Bosnia the British troops of SFOR use a British-designed vehicle called Aardvark which is a wheeled and tracked mine flail to try to clear the huge minefields laid in that conflict.

not been reached on the type of weapon to be mounted. The project was considered to be a low priority and was cancelled in April 1949.

FV206

Yet another of the ideas that seemed to abound in the period just after the war, this design is reputed to have been influenced by the German Army mounting high-velocity weapons in common obsolete chassis. It was decided to see if there was a requirement for a self-propelled gun of that type. The resulting vehicle was reputed to resemble the Brummbar, with a ball-mounted weapon in the glacis plate. Development was given a very low priority and by July 1948 it had been cancelled.

FV207

This again was an attempt to provide a self-propelled gun, but this time it was proposed that the weapon should be a 6-in (152mm) weapon. This was another low priority vehicle and had been cancelled by July 1948.

FV208

Designed as the universal Bridgelayer, it was originally hoped that the hull could be based on the hull of the FV203, although it was felt that the hull of FV202 was more suitable for the role. Originally, the bridge was to be carried flat side down, similar to the bridge deployed on the Churchill Bridgelayer. However, after trials using a mock-up bridge carried on a Centurion, it was found that the bridge fouled the ground when going cross-country. It was therefore decided that the bridge would be carried inverted, although the proposed launch system remained unaltered. To complicate matters, the final design had the bridge carried inverted and then turned over on the ground by a complex new launch system that pivoted the bridge on the ground

ahead of the vehicle. The bridge was to be 50ft (15m) class 70 with a hydraulic launch mechanism. The hull for FV208 was under construction by the end of 1949 and was then to be passed for trials and bridge construction on completion. However, no further mention of the project occurs. The final design for the bridge was transferred unaltered to Centurion and became FV4002.

FV209

This was designed to be the universal ARV. The project was cancelled, but one prototype was used for FV219 winch development. FV219 was to be developed from this vehicle on the FV214 hull by October 1950. It was later modified for trials on the FV222 winch controls development. The Nuffield mechanization and Aero organization originally designed it, with responsibility passing to Vickers around the end of 1949. If the vehicle was to be used in a DD role it was found that the rear spade earth anchor, used to help in winching, could not be fitted. This led to the investigation of fitting a front-mounted blade. This actually bore fruit years later with the Chieftain ARV having a front-mounted blade. The basis of the hull was again the FV203, which was similar to the later FV222; the lifting driver's seat and controls were to be employed. A mock-up had been completed for viewing by July 1948 and the contract to build the prototype was placed in October 1948. This was built from mild steel by Vickers and was completed and running by December 1951. However, it required modification and as always there were delays in obtaining parts, in this case parts for the winch. The vehicle was despatched to Chertsey for further trials in September 1952 and by June 1953 it had been fitted with the latest gearbox and was ready for trials, which were running in 1953. In June 1956 the vehicle was being modified to accept the much simplified control and drive equipment destined for the FV222.

FV210\211

These were to be medium and heavy artillery tractors respectively and were both accorded a low priority; both were cancelled in July 1948.

FV212

It had been proposed to use the hull of FV203 as the basis for an armoured assault personnel carrier, as at that time the British Army was still tied to the use of half-tracks or moving its infantry around in the back of soft-skin trucks. The Director of Infantry greeted the initial idea with great enthusiasm, but this eventually waned and other proposals to produce an APC were being put forward, and the project was cancelled in April 1949.

FV213

Although this vehicle had not been part of the original FV200 series it was added to the list during July 1948. The Beach Armoured Recovery Vehicle (BARV) was to be based on the hull of FV209 fitted with a flat-pack deep-wading kit, but like most of the variants it was placed on a low priority and was eventually cancelled in April 1949.

The nightmare on tracks, the FV215B. This would have indeed been a nightmare if it had entered service. Carrying the 180mm gun mounted in a thinly armoured turret mounted on FV200 components, it only reached the wooden mock-up stage. Tank Museum.

Side view of what was hoped to be the ARV for the FV200 series, its similarity to the later FV222 Mk II Conqueror ARV is very apparent. DERA Chertsey.

FV214

Heavy Gun Tank No. 1 Conqueror

FV215A

Originally this was classed as FV215, but was reclassified as FV215A to avoid confusion with the next vehicle, which had for some reason also been allocated the 215 number. FV215A was to be a heavy AVRE fitted with a mine roller. It was to combine the roles of FV202\203, apart from that of bridging, and was introduced in October 1949. It was proposed to arm it with the same 6.5in (165mm) demolition gun in possibly a limited traverse turret. It was cancelled in April 1950 in favour of the Centurion AVRE and the turret was transferred to that vehicle.

FV215B

Probably the most bizarre variant proposed must be this vehicle, which had been proposed in June 1949 as an interim vehicle for the period 1957–60. It was also sometimes known as heavy gun tank no. 2.

Morris motors carried out detailed investigations on such a vehicle during 1950. The outcome was that there were two simple methods of mounting a 180mm (7in) gun on a vehicle. To enable the gun to be brought into service as soon as possible, an interim vehicle could be constructed on a Centurion hull. Work on the Centurion version started and three trial vehicles were built. Vickers had completed a report proposing the concept of FV215B in 1951 and a contract was placed with them in June 1954 for the prototype vehicle. In March 1955 the order had been increased to include two pre-production vehicles and a fire-at trial vehicle. The mock-up was half completed by July 1955 and this was built to user acceptance standards. In January 1957 it was reported that the mock-up was complete and the drawings were 80 per cent complete. P1 was given a target date for completion in 1957, and work was in hand on this version when the project was cancelled. Also, both pre-production vehicles were cancelled, although no work had been commenced on them. The main reason for the cancellation was that by now serious doubts had been raised as to the real value of proceeding with a weapon like this, as a lot of people could see that it was going to be of very limited value tactically with its limited ammunition load. The vehicle consisted of a massive slab-sided turret mounted at the rear of the vehicle. The gearbox and engine were placed in the front of the hull. It was also proposed that the engine would be in the front and the gearbox at the rear. This was all built on a very heavily modified Caernarvon hull. Traverse of the full 360 degrees was provided, but firing was only allowed over a very limited arc. If the vehicle had fired with the gun over the side it is almost certain that the forces from the 180mm would have knocked it onto its side. Surprisingly for an armoured vehicle that was to be used in the anti-tank role only HESH was provided. The main aim of this was to produce a weapon capable of destroying anything on the battlefield by disruption only. After the project was cancelled in early 1957 development work was carried on with Centurion, producing one vehicle with an exposed gun and the other turreted.

The popular story as to why it was cancelled features the Chief of the General Staff of the day, who on being shown the mock up is reputed to have said, 'you build that over my dead body'. This was probably the wisest decision taken for a long time in the FV200 series. Those who would later detract from Conqueror by saying it was too heavy and too large for the battlefield would surely have had a field day with FV215B, weighing in at 80 tons (81,280kg), with only limited fields of fire and in relation to its size only a tiny ammunition load. In August 1957 it was finally reported that the mock-up had been scrapped and the drawings placed on file. The same gun was in fact also mounted in Centurion in a high slab-sided turret and one weapon fired a total of 150 rounds. This project was also doomed and one gun survives at the Royal Military College of Science and a turret and gun are also at the Bovington Tank Museum outside on the grassed area. Surprisingly, when one looks at them lying there they do not appear as big as we are led to believe, but the decision to cancel was the correct one as to carry on would only have diverted resources away from the rest of the projects. The drawings were reported to have been completed 'just in case' and must be hidden away till this day in some archive.

FV216

This was to be the dedicated RE mine flail with no main armament and a separate flail engine, the replacement for FV204. The idea was introduced in October 1949 but already thoughts were turning to mounting the equipment on Centurion, and therefore FV216's cancellation in April 1950 was no surprise. The Centurion version never saw the light of day and an interim version based rather unsuccessfully on the Churchill appeared briefly and then was quietly forgotten. The flail principles were revived during the Gulf War in the form of the Aardvark flail, which has also now seen service in Bosnia.

FV217

This was also known as the self-propelled 120mm medium anti-tank No. 1. This vehicle was yet another plan to get the 120mm into service as soon as possible and some reports state that it was also to have been armed with the American 155mm tank gun. This had been agreed at a tripartite meeting. It was also suggested to create a similar project based on Centurion. The vehicle was to have a low silhouette, a lighter weight and a much lower cost than any of the present alternatives to getting the 120mm into service. It was suggested that the weapon could be mounted in a limited traverse mounting of about 30 degrees either side of the centre line. This was found to be impracticable due to the need to be able to track targets, and also made it harder to take up good fire positions. The concept was proposed in May 1952 but by November 1952 the project had joined a lot of others by being cancelled.

FV218

This designation is not known to have been used for any vehicle.

FV219

Conqueror ARV Mk I was developed from the proposed FV209 on an FV214-based hull. It was realized early on in the Conqueror programme that the Centurion ARV then coming into service was just not going to be able to cope with the very large weight of Conqueror. So a specialist ARV was to be designed using as many common components as possible to ease design and keep costs down. In March 1953 it was proposed that three vehicles should be built to support the intended FV214 troop trial vehicles, giving a ratio of 1 to 7. Vickers had started work on the first ten vehicles by March 1954, and by September 1954 the order had risen to twenty vehicles with delivery to commence in January 1955. However, faults in the winch system delayed production and development, and only three vehicles were ready by September 1955. These were P1, P2 and P3. Full production of the remainder was complete by September 1959. Of these, possibly up to ten vehicles started life on the production line as FV219 but were completed as FV222, the Mk II ARV. The FV219 mock-up was inspected in June 1953 and subject to some minor modifications was accepted for development. P1 began trials in June 1955 and was in use right through till July 1956. It then had the winch removed and sent to Vickers for further development and improvements. Trials with this vehicle recommenced in August 1957 until November of the same year when the vehicle was

An excellent shot of the armoured might of BAOR on parade for Her Majesty the Queen's birthday parade at Sennelager, West Germany. Three Conqueror ARVs drive round the circuit with two Mk II vehicles closest to the camera and a Mk I on the far side. From this shot it is easy to see the differences in both vehicles. Soldier *magazine.*

handed to REME for evaluation. After this, it was sent back to Vickers where it seems to have faded away from the story.

P2 was built with all the latest modifications embedded in it and sent to the REME for winch trials in August 1957, and the same was true of P3. In August 1958, the first production standard vehicle had completed trials in recovery at the Fighting Vehicle Research Development Establishment and had been then sent to the REME at Bordon. Looking at Vickers' records for the FV219 shows that only eight were actually built, although as we have seen more were started but converted on the assembly line. This was due to the fact that the FV222 was showing itself to be by far the better vehicle.

FV220

This was another designation that does not seem to have been used.

FV221

Medium gun tank No. 1 Caernarvon. We have already studied the history of this vehicle in earlier chapters, but it is worth having a look at what vehicles were built and what happened to them before they were converted.

After all the orders and increased orders for FV221, the final total built was only ten. They were all built at the ROF at Barnbow in Leeds, with a unit cost of about £30,000. They were all built under contracts 6/FV3219 with vehicle numbers from 07 BA 68–07 BA 77. Ballast turrets which brought the all-up vehicle weight to 65 tons (66,040kg) were fitted to 07 BA 68–07 BA 72. The Centurion Mk III turrets were fitted to 07 BA 73–07 BA 77, all with a 20-pounder gun. The trial establishment at Chertsey received 07 BA 68 P5, 07 BA 69 P6 and 07 BA 70 P7. The RAC centre itself was allocated 07 BA 77 and 07 BA 72, while 07 BA 71, 07 BA 76 were sent to the 8th RTR in BAOR, 07 BA 74 and 07 BA 75 were allocated to the 14/20th Hussars and took part in the hot weather trials in Middle East Land Forces (MELF). The Ministry of supply retained 07 BA 73. Later on, seven of these vehicles would be sent to ROF Dalmuir in Scotland to be rebuilt into the latest mark of Conqueror receiving the designation Mk II/1/H. They were hard to recognize as Mk II vehicles – because they retained their Caernarvon hulls they looked like Mk I vehicles, and the easiest way of identifying them is by the vehicle registration number. They are the only FV214

A very battered Mk I FV219 Conqueror ARV with an equally battered Churchill leaning against it on Warcop ranges. Note the three apertures for the driver's sights as on the Mk I gun tank. S. Osfield.

A rear view showing the pulley wheels for the winch and the mountings for the earth anchor. S. Osfield.

vehicles whose registration starts with 07.

P5 07 BA 68

This was built at Leeds and delivered to Chertsey in December 1952. Among the trials it was subjected to were running on a lightened track and cooling trials. During this time it went through at least two engines and four gearboxes, with two auxiliary engine changes as well. By November 1955 it had completed 8,916 miles (14,346km) and was sent to Dalmuir for a rebuild, on its return receiving the turret of FV214 P2 and being used as a target in the research into the protection of heavy tanks. This could well be the vehicle that was tested to destruction at Shoeburyness. One Conqueror there was fitted with extra armour spaced from the hull on tubes and the turret received some sloping armour, with even the lower portion of the barrel from the mantlet to the fume extractor being protected. This actually made the vehicle nearly proof against attack from 185mm (7.2in) HESH, but the weight penalty was unacceptable. The records at Chertsey do not list a vehicle number for the Conqueror used, so whether it was this one has to be an educated guess.

P6 07 BA 69

This was again a Leeds vehicle which had been delivered to Chertsey by December 1952. It also ran with the light track fitted. In its time there it used three engines and four gearboxes, and completed at least 5,500 miles (8,850km) before being sent to Dalmuir for conversion to FV214.

P7 07 BA 70

This Leeds vehicle was also at Chertsey by December 1952, up-weighted and ballast-turret fitted for reliability trials; at 2,236 miles (3,598km) it had had one engine and five gearboxes. By August 1954 the hull had been drastically modified to accept the Parsons gas turbine. The vehicle ended up at Christchurch converted to a dynamometer vehicle, before finally ending up at the Bovington Tank Museum as a commentary box painted in the most lurid colours – a sad fate for a British first.

Nearly there, the final step before Conqueror made it to service was the FV221 Caernarvon. Seen here at Bovington – note the Centurion turret and 20-pounder barrel without a fume extractor, and the slack track at the front of the vehicle. Tank Museum.

P8 07 BA 71

This was one of the vehicles that was sent to the 8th RTR for user trials. Whilst with the Regiment it received the name Hengist, and by July 1954 it had completed 1,037 miles (1,670km). No record is known of how many engines and gearboxes were used. The vehicle was then returned to the UK and in November 1956 it ran with the Rolls Royce M120 engine which was an experimental engine using a lot of light alloy steels. From there it was sent to be converted to FV214.

P9 07 BA 72

This vehicle seems to have had a very uneventful life. It was at Bovington for user trials on project 1001B, then later sent to Dalmuir and converted to FV214.

07 BA 73

This pre-production model was kept for trial by the Ministry of Supply, then, nothing more is known.

07 BA 71 P8 at an unidentified location, showing well how by now the final design had taken shape on what was to be Conqueror. This shows to good effect the Windsor turret fitted in place of the service turret. Notice on the top of the turret the mounting for adding weight so that the vehicle can be run under simulated weight of its final all-up weight. Tank Museum.

07 BA 74

This pre-production model was sent to MELF, then converted to Conqueror.

07 BA 75

This pre-production model was also sent to MELF. On its return to the UK the vehicle was reworked at FVRDE workshops to FV214 standards.

07 BA 76

This pre-production model was sent to 8th RTR. It was named Horsa for BAOR troop trials and also became an FV214.

07 BA 77

This was another pre-production vehicle sent to Bovington, then to conversion. As can be seen, the pre-production vehicles had varied and interesting lives, with some longer than others. We do sometimes have a tendency to forget all about the trials and research that occur before a vehicle actually takes its place within the forces.

FV222

This vehicle was also known as armoured recovery vehicle Mk II, and was originally meant to be developed in parallel with the Centurion Mk III ARV, which was, in the event, not proceeded with. The vehicle first appears to have been mentioned around July 1955 when it was decided that the vehicle would go straight into production without any prototypes being constructed. This in itself was a very bold move, but one that for once paid off very well.

The FV222 user saw the first mock-up at a meeting in October 1955 and the design was approved, thus allowing work to start on finalizing the drawings. In August 1957 the drawings were complete enough to allow production to start as soon as the order was received. All of the winch modifications from FV219 were to be incorporated. Full production of FV222 began in September 1959 and by 1960 production vehicles were entering service. The layout of the vehicle was unusual in that the driver was situated in the crew compartment rather than the normal isolated location at the front of the vehicle. The main difference between the two ARVs was that the Mk II looked as if it had been designed right from the start as an ARV, rather than having the converted look of the Mk I.

With its long sloping glacis plate, it bore a resemblance to the earlier FV200 AVRE. A novel innovation with this vehicle was that when the driver wished to drive closed down instead of just lowering his seat as on the Mk I, the whole driver's compartment floor was lowered including the steering levers and all the controls. These were mounted on special linkages, designed to allow this to take place. As an ARV the vehicle was very popular due to its immense recovery capability, and also to the fact that ARVs tended not to break down quite so often as the gun tanks. One Mr Vernon, who was a WO with 4th/7th RDG REME, served on the FV222 and has nothing but praise for the vehicle. As mentioned earlier, some idea of the power of these vehicles can be judged in that a Conqueror was the only vehicle with enough strength to move dead Shir tanks about during the development of Challenger. It is only with the advent of the Challenger Repair and Recovery Vehicle that such a powerful vehicle is now back on the inventory of the British Army. Two working examples can still be seen today at Duxford and Bordon with the REME, and if you are lucky to see them it is well worth the visit. There is also talk that a third may be recovered from a firing range and restored – one can only hope! One other surviving FV222 served at Bordon as a recovery aid, being winched out of a waterlogged hole and then pushed back ready for the next time, before being bought by Mr D. Arnold for restoration.

A very nicely preserved Mk II Conqueror ARV. This one belongs to the REME museum of historic vehicles at Bordon and is a working exhibit. Author.

FV223

This is the last variant that was suggested. It was proposed when it was found that the long-term availability of hulls for the Churchill-linked ARK was in doubt. The linked ARK consisted of two Churchill ARKs joined together and they were driven side by side – a bizarre solution aimed to create an ARK that could handle Conqueror. The FV223 was

Another lucky survivor, this Mk II spent a lot of its days working at the Proof Establishment at Shoeburyness before being saved and transferred to the hands of Duxford armour wing of the Imperial War Museum. It had been planned to send it down range as a hard target by a soulless government accountant. Luckily sense prevailed, and today it is another working exhibit. P&EE Shoeburyness.

What appears to be a not so lucky survivor, Mk II ARV on the ranges. This vehicle is now owned by Mr D. Arnold and is to be fully restored. S. Osfield.

This Mk II ARV was used as a recovery aid by the REME at Bordon, but has now been bought by Mr D. Arnold for full restoration. Author.

probably to be based on an FV214 hull or on a Centurion, although at first it was thought that the weight would be impracticable for Centurion and so work was concentrated on Conqueror. However, with the advance of light alloys the scheme was moved to Centurion and in that guise finally entered service, leaving the FV223 to be cancelled by August 1958.

A specification had been issued to produce a medium anti-aircraft SP weapon based on the FV200 series. However, no designation was ever issued, and like so many of the grand schemes for the FV200 series it disappeared, leaving FV219 and FV222 as the only Conqueror variants actually to make it into service.

It is worth looking at the numbering of the FV200 series as it is, to say the least, not logical. When the system of numbering vehicles was changed so that those groups would all sit in the same class this is what should have happened to the listing of the FV200 series. However, it would

appear that there were at least two methods of numbering with one not aware of the other. One appears to have been a chronological order, while the other follows the original FV200 numbering. The first vehicles to be given numbers would have been FV214, FV215, FV215A and FV216, all following in a chronological order. But then Caernarvon appeared and it seems to have retained the last digit of the original gun tank FV201, thus becoming FV221. This also seems to have occurred with the ARV retaining the 9 of the FV209 and becoming FV219. Similarly, FV215 retains the 5 from the original anti-tank project. From here on the numbers were applied at random or so it would seem, coming first was FV217 followed by FV216, while the allocations of FV218 and FV220 were never used as far as is known, not even for obscure projects. This does make for a lot of confusion when one is trying to trace information on the FV200 series.

7 Gas Turbine

We have seen the designer of any armoured fighting vehicle has to work within tight parameters based on firepower, mobility and protection. Any increase in one of these can have an adverse affect on the other two. Designers know that armour must be the best that can be employed, just as the gun must be of a sufficient calibre to cope with any advances in the enemy's designs. This only leaves mobility with which to experiment and try to achieve something innovative. For example, if an engine could be developed that would give the same power output but would weigh less, then perhaps the weight saved would allow for extra armour or more ammunition. However, from the very first days of the tank in World War I the only means of powering the vehicle was the very low output petrol engines of the day. In World War II, at least in Britain, the petrol engine still reigned supreme, while in Russia notably the diesel engine was rapidly becoming the main power plant for the AFV. Thus even at the end of the war only two main sources were in existence as power plants, partly due to the limitations of materials and knowledge, but also because in a war the attitudes tends to be one of 'if it's not broken, don't fix it'. This is not to level a criticism at designers, merely to point out that it may not have been the best time for radical new ideas.

Despite this, there were in fact many ideas floating around at the close of the war. One such idea was the gas turbine; its champion was Sir Frank Whittle, who ultimately developed Britain's first jet aircraft. The ultimate aim of the gas turbine was to get a new engine into the skies that would be lighter, produce more power and thus greater speed. However, the importance of the gas turbine was not lost on AFV designers and after many struggles, at 1430 hours on 30 September 1954 at its first public display Conqueror prototype P7 (ex 07 BA 70) made AFV history by becoming the first heavy tracked vehicle in the world to be propelled by a gas-turbine engine. This was a feat not repeated until the public showing of both M1 Abrams contenders for the new American MBT contract on 3 February 1976.

However, in true British form this world-beating episode has never been given the recognition that it surely deserves. Even the history-making vehicle has been reduced to being used as a commentary box at the Tank Museum at Bovington, rather than being preserved as the milestone in development that it represents. But if we look at the reasoning behind the gas-turbine project then we can perhaps understand why this has happened.

HISTORY OF THE GAS TURBINE

Let us first take a look at exactly what a gas turbine is and see whether all the claims that were made for it as a viable alternative engine for armoured vehicles were justified. The theory of turbines and gas-turbine engines, like many modern inventions, was not a particularly new idea, with a turbine defined as 'an engine providing direct rotary motion by the dynamic action of a fluid on some form of paddle wheel or fan'. Whilst that may overly simplify the theory, it does give an indication of what turbine theory is based on. A windmill might be described as a gas (or air) turbine, and a watermill as a hydraulic (or water) turbine.

However, the term is usually applied to more sophisticated devices that apply the same principles using hot expanding gases, steam or falling water to provide the power. While we tend to think of the turbine as a fairly modern invention, the first recorded example of a jet engine or turbine in fact can be traced back to 150BC. An Egyptian inventor named Hero made what was in essence a toy that rotated on top of a boiling pot due to the reaction of hot air or steam exiting several nozzles arranged radially around a sphere. He called his invention an 'aeolpile'.

In 1232 the Chinese used a rudimentary form of rocket in battle to frighten enemy soldiers. In AD1500 Leonardo da Vinci drew a sketch of a device that rotated due to the effect of hot gases flowing up a chimney. The device was intended to be used to rotate meat being roasted. In 1629 another Italian by the name of Giovanni Branca actually developed a device that used jets of steam to rotate a turbine that in turn was used to operate machinery. This is probably the first recorded practical use of a turbine. Ferdinand Verbiest, a Jesuit in China, built a model carriage that used a steam jet for power in 1678.

There are many more recorded examples of early turbine engines by various inventors, but none can be considered true gas turbines because of their use of steam in the operation. However, these early examples show that the basic theory of producing a gas turbine was understood a long time ago.

In 1791 the world's first patent for a gas turbine was granted to the Englishman John Barber. It incorporated many of the same elements of a modern gas turbine, but used a reciprocating compressor. However, he encountered the problems that still exist today but in greater form, and without our sophisticated technology to help him. His main problem was that of trying to find the ideal material with which to construct the engine, for, as we shall see later, high temperature is a requirement for successful turbine operation. In 1872 a man by the name of Stolze designed the first true gas turbine. His engine incorporated a multi-stage turbine section and a multi-stage axial flow compressor. He

had working models running in the early 1890s.

The man who probably brought the turbine to prominence was the English engineer Charles Parsons, 1854–1931. He came from an engineering background and as a boy was a great model maker. He went to Cambridge to study engineering and then found employment in a firm in Leeds. Around this time, the battle for speed between liners on the Atlantic crossing had started and the speed of 24 knots was nearing the limit for a conventional reciprocating steam engine. He saw that the movement of heavy pistons and rods in fact wasted energy and set himself the task of inventing an engine where the parts turned contiguously. He knew the history of the early attempts at this type of engine and also knew that men like James Watt and Richard Trevithick had experimented along these lines. However, like the early inventors they had tended to rely on steam being blown onto blades to cause movement. Parsons saw little use for this type of engine and set about producing his own turbine. This was completed in 1884 and was used to drive a dynamo. He also designed a turbine that was installed in the Cambridge electrical power station. His mind was still occupied, however, with the aim of harnessing the power of his turbine for the propulsion of a vessel. He designed and built the *Turbinia* of 100ft (30m) length with a beam of 9ft (2.7m). The hull was almost filled with a steam turbine engine developing some 2000hp. On trials it achieved a speed of 32 knots. On offering it to the British Royal Navy Parsons was met with total indifference. He decided that the only way to get his invention noticed would be to create a major disturbance in the grand old order. This he did to great effect in 1897 during the great naval review held at Spithead to celebrate Queen Victoria's Diamond jubilee. Parsons and *Turbinia* suddenly appeared in the middle of the ceremony and he wove in and out of the gathered warships and easily evaded the entire Royal Navy's attempts to catch him. This had the desired effect and in 1898 the Royal Navy took delivery of its first steam turbine powered ship. The company that Parsons formed will feature later on in our look at turbines.

In 1897 the Swedish engineer Nils Gustaf Dalen invited a friend of his to partner him in the construction of what was in essence a turbine, although nothing more is heard of them after that initial contact. Six years later, a German named Hans Holzwarth patented an engine which he called an 'explosion turbine'. The very first unit built to his specification was completed at Hanover in 1908. He then cooperated with the company of Brown-Boveri in Mannheim to produce a gas turbine rated at 1,000hp. However, the prototype of this even when running at full power only produced 200hp. It is interesting to note that Brown-Boveri continued to develop this engine up till 1933.

Meanwhile in the United States Charles Curtis, the inventor of the Curtis steam engine, filed the first patent application for a gas turbine in the US. This was granted in 1914. Also in the US the General Electric Company started their turbine division in 1903 led by an engineer by the name of Stanford Moss. His most outstanding development was that of the turbosupercharger during World War I, although credit for this is usually attributed to Rateu of France.

In the United Kingdom work had carried on after Parsons' success, but by now interest lay in using other forms of turbine as steam has obvious limitations. Although several companies had been working on designs and the idea of propelling an aircraft by the use of a gas turbine had been put forward, not for the first time did little official interest occur. The Air Ministry came up with the figures (1920) that a piston engine of the type then in use would operate on a weight of fuel of 1kg/hp against projected figures for the turbine of 2.7kg/hp. The firm of Bristol's had been working on turbochargers, which form part of a turbine, since 1923, but it totally ignored gas turbines until 1940.

At the Royal Aircraft Establishment A. Griffith developed a turbine, but like a lot of his work it was exceedingly complex and way ahead of its time, so it too was cancelled in 1929. The most famous British person connected with the development of the gas turbine now appeared on the scene, Sir Frank Whittle. Whittle had written a paper on the gas turbine in 1928 and although he was allowed to continue the investigation of the theory no government interest was forthcoming as no military use could be envisaged for the new engine. The lack of interest even extended to allowing Whittle to publish his papers on gas-turbine theory. He patented the basics of a working gas turbine in January 1930, but due to the lack of encouragement it was never renewed. In 1936 Whittle formed a company in conjunction with Williams and Tinling, which was to be called Power Jets Ltd. On a shoestring budget it had its first engine ready to run by 1937. In 1939, with the war clouds looming, interest was taken in Whittle's invention and he was awarded a development contract from the Air Ministry which meant that money would become available for research and development.

In Germany, interest in gas turbines continued. In 1920 Ludwig Prandtl had become involved in the study of airflow especially concerning aerofoils. He then applied this theory to increasing the efficiency of turbines and compressors. As always in any new development, it was not long before argument about who built what appeared, and the gas-turbine story is no different, for in Göttingen Hans Pabst von Ohain and Max Hein designed, built and then patented an engine that was similar to Whittle's, although it differed in some details. Their work was taken up by the Ernst Heinkel company. Ohain claimed that he had never heard of the Englishman Whittle and all his work was his own invention; however, his colleagues contradicted that statement. Controversy over plagiarism notwithstanding Ohain did produce a turbine and in May 1939 it flew for the first time beneath an HE 118. On 27 August 1939 the first true jet flight took place with the engine in an HE 178. Although the engine worked the airframe was an aerodynamic disaster and it rarely flew again, but it had given Germany the first flight ever of a gas-turbine-powered aircraft. The Heinkel HES-3b engine generated 1,100lb (500kg) of thrust and flew at over 400mph (644km/h). This would lead later to the ME 262 fighter capable of 500mph (805km/h) plus.

This led the Air Ministry to push for a British fighter to catch up in the race for jet aircraft and suddenly Whittle was acceptable. The first British jet plane was the Gloster E28.39, which flew from Brockworth airfield in Gloucester in May 1941. This was a vastly inferior aircraft to its German competitor, but at least it was a start, and by the end of the war the more successful Gloster *Meteor* was in the skies and destroying the German flying bombs.

In Germany Junkers also had been working on a secret gas turbine before July 1936 and the engine ran in 1938. This programme was conducted in great secrecy, which was nothing unusual in Nazi Germany at that time, but the reason this time was that the engine had been produced by the airframe section of Junkers and not, as one would expect, by the engine department. The latter were considered by the remainder of the company to be totally unadventurous. From this point onwards, the gas-turbine development in both Germany and the UK took on a greater role with both countries producing operational aircraft by the end of the war.

The ending of the war and the subsequent capture of equipment and documents and probably most important of all the capture of the German scientists and engineers, provided the UK with a tremendous insight into how far advanced the Germans had been with gas-turbine technology. It was seen that where most schools of thought had envisaged the turbine as means of aircraft propulsion, the Germans were looking at using it to power their AFVs at the end of the war. This project had the backing of the *Waffen* SS and it was hoped to be able to produce an engine in the region of 1,000hp to fit into the *Panzer* IIs of the SS that were on the drawing board for production around 1945–6 if the war had carried on.

The reasoning for the flurry of design activity was seen as partly political in the ongoing bitter rivalry between the *Wermacht* and SS and in part the hope of creating an engine that could reap the advantages then claimed for gas turbines. These were improved performance, lighter weight, low cost, the ability to use low-grade fuels, a

simplification of the transmission, no cooling requirement easy starting in cold conditions (as many bitter lessons had been learnt during the Eastern front campaigns), and a less rigid air cleaner requirement.

These claims are all to some extent still valid today and must have looked very attractive to a country struggling to survive in the later stages of the war.

In November 1948, the power branch of FVRDE raised a report on the Germans' use of gas turbines in tanks, which led to the award in January of a contract to construct a gas-turbine engine to C. A. Parsons based in Newcastle. The engine was to be used to propel an AFV and it was to be capable of developing 1,000bhp at 60°F and 900bhp at 110°F. By this time there were several types of gas turbine to choose from, with each version having advantages and disadvantages. In the end, it was decided to look at the construction of a simple cycle with a centrifugal compressor driven by a single-stage turbine in series with a two-stage work turbine.

We will now look as simply as possible at the operation of a gas turbine and to see if it does have any advantages over more conventional types of engine. Like the petrol and diesel engine the gas turbine has its own cycle of operation, which is called the Brayton cycle. This exists in two forms – the open cycle and the closed cycle; however, the open cycle is not a true cycle, and so it is the closed cycle that we are going to look at.

THE GAS-TURBINE ENGINE

In an open cycle, air is compressed by a rotary compressor, thus the air temperature created is raised by combustion with the fuel. This causes the air to expand and the products of this expansion are discharged and the power output of the exhaust gases is either harnessed as a straight propulsion system, as in a turbojet or by a turbine driven by the expanding gases, such as a turboprop, static engine or in an automotive power unit.

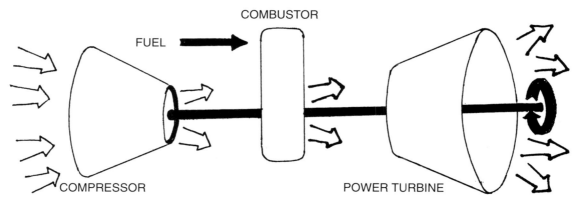

FUEL

COMBUSTOR

COMPRESSOR

POWER TURBINE

Simple gas turbine.

For those brought up on conventional engines the operation of the gas turbine must be a contradiction in terms, for where they have spent time ensuring that their engine does not run beyond a certain temperature, the operation of the turbine is contrary to that. The overall efficiency of the engine is conditioned by the operating temperature and the higher the operating temperature the greater the overall efficiency for a given power output. More importantly for vehicle designers, the unit can be made smaller, thus hopefully leaving space for other equipment or fuel.

In the early days, designers were hampered by the lack of suitable alloys and engineering techniques from which to construct the engines, thus the temperatures achieved were never those that the design teams would have liked. One way of improving the efficiency of the early gas turbines was by the inclusion of a heat exchanger, which used the exhaust gases to heat the compressed air from the compressor prior to combustion. The problem in employing a heat exchanger was that it was required to operate at high combustion temperatures and this caused difficulty with the design and manufacture of the early heat exchangers.

Let's now look briefly at the main components that make up a typical gas turbine.

The Compressor

These were built in two forms – either centrifugal, sometimes called a radial compressor, or the axial type. In the early days of British development Whittle used the centrifugal, while Griffiths used the axial. The Germans also preferred the axial layout. The job of the compressor as we have seen is to compress the airflow and to raise the temperature before the introduction of the fuel. The main difference between the two types is that the centrifugal has a cone-shaped disc fitted with radial cones and the air is radiated outwards by centrifugal force into an annular diffuser, which converts the velocity of air flow into air pressure. The early Rolls Royce engines, such as the Nene, used this system.

The axial compressor consists of a disc with angled blades extending from the circumference and it is this type of blade arrangement that we are used to seeing in drawings of turbines.

The compressor was built as a single-stage unit, but more often with the axial type as a multi-stage unit with rows of stationary blades known as stators after each rotating stage. Out of interest, the pressures achieved in these early stages amounted to about 2.5:1–1.5:1, whereas the RB199 engine from the Tornado has a ratio of about 2:3.

Combustion Chamber

The combustion chamber as used on the Parsons turbine was a cylinder usually of double skin construction and it was within this component that the burner was located and also the mixture of fuel and air was burned. The main object of the combustion chamber was to provide a continuous flow of gas to the turbine that was uniform in temperature. Air was fed into the chamber through holes around the burner. The spray of fuel had to be vaporized and the airflow assisted in that. Part of the flow of air was directed between the two skins to aid in cooling – as part of the attraction of a gas-turbine power system was that there was no need for an external cooling system as was common on vehicles at that time. Unfortunately, combustion chambers tended to be longer than the ideal length that was available between the compressor and the turbine.

The Turbine

The heart of the engine was the turbine itself. As we have seen, the idea of a turbine is not new and has been used by hydroelectric engineers for many years, and you can even find turbines in use in our homes in the shower heads which give a variety of speeds and settings. In its simplest form, a turbine is simply a propeller whose blades are turned by a force hitting them. That force can be water as in hydroelectric generators and shower heads, wind as in windmills, steam, or in our case gas from the burnt fuel being directed onto the vanes of the turbine. It was decided that the turbine that would be developed for use in AFVs would be of the axial type. It would also be multi-staged with the majority of energy passing into the turbine which was required to drive the compressor. In a turbojet engine the turbine was a lot smaller as the additional energy was used in the form of air velocity to power the aircraft, with the turbine only required to drive the compressor.

A turboprop or vehicle turbine has a large turbine that converts as much as possible of the exhaust gases into usable energy in the form of rotary

power. However, whilst creating the right operating temperatures the super heat of the exhaust could be more than required, especially on an AFV, and so it was planned that as much of the energy as possible would be extracted before the exhaust. Using the compressor turbine to provide the power output was not all that simple in an automotive environment, as the little torque would be provided at low rpm. This would mean the production of a complex transmission system. It also would mean that the whole compressor turbine would be continually accelerated and decelerated as part of normal driving conditions. This was unlike its use in an aircraft, where once take-off and maximum flying speed had been achieved the engine would be maintained at fairly constant revolutions. It was decided that a separate work turbine could be included, which would allow the compressor turbine to drive only the compressor while the work turbine provided the rotary power for propulsion. This rotary power could then be transmitted to a gearbox to provide drive to the vehicle. The Conqueror which was fitted with the gas turbine retained its original gearbox, although the plan, if the system had ever gone into production, was to take advantage of the torque available from the gas-turbine engine to design a transmission that was both simpler in design and was produced entirely for a gas-turbine vehicle. In this case the compressor turbine unit acted as a gas producer for the work turbine. With the work turbine stalled, i.e. with a vehicle held on its brakes and maximum RPM from the gas producer section, considerable torque multiplication would be available (about 2.5:1), permitting a simpler transmission design.

Heat Exchanger

A heat exchanger was fitted to increase the temperature of the air before it was allowed to enter the combustion chamber; this was to reduce the quantity of fuel required to bring the air to the required working temperature. Two types of heat exchanger were available. One was the steady flow system alternatively known as the recuperator, in which the two gas streams were separated by a wall across which the heat must be transferred. The other was the periodic flow type, also known as a regenerator. In this type a rotating heat transfer matrix was exposed alternately to the hot and cold gas streams. The matrix retained the heat from the exhaust and then transferred it to the unheated compressed air. This type was found to be in general the most efficient both in its transfer of heat and in its volume requirements, although against that was its more complex design and requirement for a drive linked to the compressor turbine shaft. Another problem encountered was the creation of an airtight sealing system and this relegated the use of regenerator-type heat exchangers to engines with low-pressure ratios.

Starting

Gas turbines were started by one of two methods, either by means of a starter cartridge as used on aircraft or by means of an electrical starter motor. Spark plug type igniters were supplied to initiate combustion during the start-up process. If, as on the Parsons' turbine an electric starter was used, then a starter control board was fitted. This contained a time switch that controlled all of the necessary functions for start-up in the required order and at the correct time. Once the engine was running the starter motor disengaged and the board automatically reset itself ready for the next time that it would be required.

MANUFACTURING MATERIALS

Covered above are the basic components of a gas turbine, and especially of the period during which Conqueror was fitted with one. As science has moved on, the problems that befell the early gas-turbine engine have now been overcome, although the gas turbine remains a complicated engine and is therefore not a common power pack for use in AFVs.

One of the early difficulties experienced by

A sectioned gas turbine in the Tank Museum at Bovington. This is in fact an amalgam of two engines to make one and then sectioned. The whereabouts of the gas turbines used for the trials is still something of a mystery, with no one admitting to their ultimate fate. Author.

companies involved in the manufacture of gas turbines and turbochargers was the provision of a suitable material from which to make the turbine. Aircraft turbocharger technology was used to assist the early gas-turbine programmes, as the turbine in both cases had to be capable of continuous operation at very high temperatures. As we have seen already, the higher the temperature the more efficient the engine's operation.

One solution to this problem of material was the introduction of compressed air into the turbine to cool it. There was some loss of efficiency, but it allowed the materials then available to be used reasonably effectively. In 1939 the Germans had tried ceramic blades in temperatures as high as 9,000°C, but the blades failed and air-cooled blades were used instead. Tungsten had also been tried, but this created a weight penalty that was not acceptable. The blade problem was not solved until the development of nimonic alloys. The performance today of gas turbines is still very much limited by the material that is available for making the turbine blades, despite sophisticated methods of air cooling and new types of materials. An example of temperatures that can be created is the Panavia Tornado which has a turbine inlet temperature of 13,270°C.

Similar problems existed with other components, not only in the choice of materials but in the field of mixing air and fuel. In those early days the process of the fuel burning was not fully understood, thus the procedure of maintaining a continuous and effective flame was still very much under development. Even today, the process is still not 100 per cent understood.

We have taken a very brief look at what is an extremely complex subject that would fill many textbooks. However, it is important that we have some understanding of the operation of a gas turbine so that we can better understand the reasons for its development to fit into Conqueror and the trials and tribulations it faced.

DEVELOPMENT OF THE GAS TURBINE

As we have seen, the requirement for experiments to try to design and fit a gas-turbine engine into a British AFV had been promulgated by the power plant branch of the Fighting Vehicle Research and Development Establishment in November 1948. The investigations which were based on the German attempt to field a 1,000hp engine in the later stages of the war led to a contract being placed with C A Parsons Ltd of Newcastle. This was to investigate the design of a gas turbine suitable to fit into an armoured vehicle. It had to be capable of developing 1,000bhp at 60°F; five members of the original German design team were part of the team, with a further two acting in an advisory capacity.

From the beginning it was clear that the requirement for a four-speed and more likely a five-speed gearbox would be necessary due to the needs of the steering system. It was hoped that this would also aid fuel economy. The vehicle chosen for the testing of the turbine was based on the FV200 series. As a benchmark, the figures obtained from the trial were to be compared to a Meteor Mk XI fuel-injected engine. Also it was to be measured against an imaginary supercharged version of the Meteor engine.

One of the first observations that came to light was that many of the claims for the gas turbine could not be met given the state of development at the time. It was found that only by using light alloys and thinner gauge materials could the gas turbine's weight be brought down to that of a conventional reciprocating engine. The figures that were originally envisaged were a turbine weight of 5,400lb (2,450kg) and reciprocating engine at 4,100lb (1,860kg). It was accepted that running costs were going to be higher for the turbine, but it was hoped that by running on lower grade fuels a happy medium might be struck. The engine was expected to be a very noisy machine and to occupy at least 25 per cent more space due to the circular construction of the engine components and the heat exchangers. This was entirely acceptable, as the trial remit was to investigate the feasibility of fitting such an engine, not the design of one to fit the AFV.

In September 1954 the first prototype Parsons gas-turbine engine serial no. 2979, in development since 1948, was ready to be fitted into an AFV. We know that it was to be fitted into an FV200 series and the vehicle chosen was one of the three Leeds ROF-built pre-production FV221 vehicles housed at Chertsey. The vehicle that was selected was 07 BA 70, later known as Conqueror prototype P7; the vehicle had been heavily modified to accept the gas turbine. Two engines were now in existence – one of 655bhp and the other of 910bhp. It was decided to accept and fit the engine with the lower bhp after a ten-hour test of the type on a dynamometer, although it had been expected that the engine would be rated at 1,000bhp. With the engine now installed the vehicle literally became a mobile test bed.

A brief mention of the turbine type fitted is appropriate now. The unit incorporated a single-stage centrifugal compressor, which was driven by a single-stage axial flow turbine. Neither the nozzles nor the rotor blades were cooled, only the turbine disc was air-cooled. The work turbine was a two-stage axial flow turbine running in series with the compressor. A reduction gear unit was fitted which reduced the speed of the work turbine from 9,960 rpm to 2,800rpm. Fuel was provided by a

The rear hull of 07 BA 70 being modified to take the gas-turbine installation. Tank Museum.

Lucas fuel pump. Lucas also supplied an air–fuel ratio control unit, incorporating in it a throttle unit. In order to prevent the work turbine from overspeeding during gear changes and to obtain engine braking, the work turbine could be connected mechanically to the compressor turbine through a freewheel.

To start the engine the compressor turbine was rotated by a 24v starter motor and the ignition was by torch igniter. Once the starter button had been pressed the sequence of starting was automatically controlled by a Rotax gas-turbine starting panel.

The clutch system employed was a four-plate dry clutch with a hydraulic servo-assisted mechanism fitted. A conventional gearbox of five speeds was fitted and Merritt-Brown steering was employed. It was necessary to lengthen the gearbox compartment to take the gearbox, but the location

of the drive sprockets stayed the same. The fighting compartment housed the cyclone air-cleaner unit, consisting of 192 cyclone units mounted in eight batteries of twenty-four. Also in the fighting compartment were the two fuel tanks and a homelite generator, which was required due to the lack of a generator drive on the gas turbine. The driver was well served with instrumentation, having no less than twenty-nine instruments to monitor. Also included was standard fire-fighting equipment, and this gave an all-up vehicle weight of 45 tons (45,720kg).

THE TRIALS

All was now in place to commence the trials, although the first most important thing was to have

The installation complete; it can be seen from this shot just how much room the turbine has taken in the vehicle. With this level of technology it would not have been possible to envisage a gun-armed variant of Conqueror. Tank Museum.

the vehicle ready for the FVRDE military vehicle display on 30 September 1954. A lot of effort went into ensuring that the vehicle was ready in time and it was completed on 3 September. On the 4th, the unit started first time, then was allowed to run for ten minutes, before having to be halted due the throttle sticking in the open position. The fault was rectified and on 9 September the vehicle was towed to the test track ready for its initial run. Although the engine had started satisfactorily on the 4th it would not accelerate past a turbine compressor speed of 2,700rpm. No obvious fault could be detected, so all the burner filters were removed and cleaned, and finally a successful start was achieved. After carrying out various checks the vehicle moved

out to the track under its own power for the first time. It set off in fourth gear and with the turbine running at 6,500rpm successfully completed one circuit of the track, taking 15 minutes to do so. As a result of this run, various components were either repaired or replaced and several joints were brazed again.

Further runs were carried out on 21 and 22 September, with a total running time of 2 hours and 3 minutes. In general, the engine performed well, although some trouble was experienced in starting, and a partial solution was found by adding four extra batteries. During a run on the 23rd when the driver tried to change from fifth to fourth gear he could not, so the vehicle was halted and the driver attempted to engage third gear but managed to engage reverse. It was then found that it was stuck in reverse so the vehicle was towed to workshops and the gearbox removed. Modifications were made and the unit reinstalled. By the afternoon of the 27th the vehicle was ready for a check run, which consisted of static checks and a short road run. This showed that the gearbox and gear changing were satisfactory, and nothing more was done as the vehicle now had to be washed and painted ready for its big day.

On 30 September 1954, P7 made its public debut and thus drove into the history books as the first heavy-tracked vehicle to be propelled by a gas-turbine power plant. The demonstration went off smoothly and the watching crowd was visibly impressed according to one of the team that day. It made another public display on the FVRDE open day for FVRDE personnel, and again had another successful run.

However, while it was found that the acceleration times were quite acceptable, it was discovered that the deceleration time was far too slow, causing problems with changing gear from low to high. Noise measurements were taken from various positions around the vehicle, as the noise produced by a healthy turbine was a new and very loud noise. The lowest level recorded was in front of the vehicle, that being the point furthest from the unit. It was felt that a maximum noise level of 92db was

The gas turbine underway driven by the late Mr Busty Sutton. The vehicle was painted unusually in silver; this may have been to help it stand out for the press day. Possibly one of the other figures in the picture may well be the Director of the then FVRDE, Mr Masters, who died in 1966. Tank Museum.

acceptable, although work would carry on to reduce this further.

The engine had now achieved a total running of 11 hours and 51 minutes, and no further running was to take place. A full strip and rebuild would now take place at FVRDE. The repairs and modifications that took place as a result of this strip fill nearly five pages of A4 paper when condensed, showing just how thorough the job was.

On 19 April 1955 the engine was reinstalled into P7 and was ready to carry on the trials, with each day being different. Some days, the engine functioned perfectly, while on others it just would not start, but this of course is what the trials were all about. By 24 May the engine was performing well and amongst its tests that day it climbed the 1 in 7

slope and 1 in 6 slope, carrying out hill starts and moving off in fifth gear. Overall, the performance was satisfactory, although a more rapid response of engine acceleration–deceleration over the whole throttle range would have improved the vehicle performance, especially the driving characteristics. On 8 June 1955 the final gas-turbine tests were carried out, consisting of warm and cold starts. These concluded the programme, having gained much valuable data.

The final results showed that the theory of putting a gas turbine into a vehicle was feasible, but a lot of design work would need to be carried out in order to reduce weight and size. It was felt that the engine performed well in P7 given that it had received only very limited test-bed running. The

The gas turbine's hull in its later working days as a dynamometer vehicle and again painted in a strange colour scheme. Notice the welded-up rear wheel station and Chieftain tank track. Author.

future test would comprise the second gas-turbine engine no. 2983 as this was rated at approximately 910bhp. The increased power output would allow P7 to be ballasted to obtain performance ratios compared to other current vehicles, and the second engine was also expected to be more reliable. The test would also pay attention to cross-country performance and the noise problem.

In March 1956 the project was taken away from Parsons and handed to FVRDE, with Parsons producing its last report on April 1955. From there on, what happened next is still clouded in secrecy, with information either having been destroyed or retained as classified.

There we end one of Conqueror's more interesting chapters in its very short life. Although some good hard data was accumulated it did not seem to convince designers that here was the

answer to all their prayers as we saw at the beginning of this chapter. Perhaps it was the need for new materials that held them back, but whatever the reason the British soldiered on with the Rolls Royce Meteor, followed by the disastrous Leyland L60 which was forced onto the Chieftain design team by a government that would not wait for Rolls Royce to develop the new engine. This left Chieftain with an embarrassing flop of a power pack. Who knows what Rolls Royce would have produced – maybe a Chieftain powered by a British gas turbine?

In the end, only two countries have embraced the gas turbine operationally, the United States and the then Soviet Union. The Americans fielded the M1 Abrams and the Russians the T80. Interestingly, both vehicles had diesel engines waiting in the wings should the gas turbine not be successful. The

The turbine's hull in yet another guise and probably its last unless someone decides to unite it inside the museum with its engine. It has now sprouted another cabin and is now used as a commentary box for two to three months of the year at the Tank Museum at Bovington, sporting what must be its worst colour scheme since it was built. Author.

Americans produced the turbine and diesel together as they knew they had a good tank in the M1, so if the turbine failed then in would go the diesel. For a time it looked like the gas turbine would fail due to problems with dust getting into the engine and damaging it; also it was criticized for being too thirsty. However, all these problems are now behind it, and as the Gulf War showed it proved to be a fine armoured vehicle. The USSR with T80 produced the diesel-engined variant as an alternative for export sale as it was felt that the turbine was too complicated for some of its customers. As to how the USSR fared with the turbine-engined version, that is still anyone's guess, but significantly the latest Russian tank, the T90, is powered by a conventional diesel engine.

From Hero in 150BC to the present day the turbine has a long history, and I believe an even longer one in front of it.

8 Finis?

We have seen all through this book that the main reason for Conqueror's existence was to supply a long-range anti-tank killing capacity to the 20-pounder-armed Centurions. It was always known that this was going to be a short-lived vehicle, as the main criterion had been to get the 120mm into service as soon as possible. To try to predict how long an AFV will remain in service is next to impossible. No-one could have possibly foretold that Centurion would have such a long service life, only leaving British service in the last few years and still soldiering on in other countries. Another example was the Ferret scout car; it was meant to be replaced by the Fox armoured car, instead of which it survived to see Fox withdrawn from service and its turrets being used on redundant Scorpion hulls to create Sabre. It had always been accepted that as soon as there was another weapon or vehicle that could carry out the tank-killing role, the demise of Conqueror would happen, a case of not if but when.

During the late sixties and early seventies a very good series of publications on AFVs was produced. These were known as Profile publications and in the one on the Conqueror the author, Major Mike Norman, who at the time was serving as Technical Adjutant with the Royal Tank Regiment, noted that with the coming of the 105mm-armed Centurion, Conqueror was swiftly withdrawn from service and put out on the ranges to be battered to scrap as hard targets, the only Conqueror remaining intact being the one in the Tank Museum. Fortunately, that is not in fact the case, with certainly more than one remaining.

To understand why Conqueror was withdrawn after such a short service life it is necessary to travel back to 1956 when the research and development of future tank guns, tank armour and ammunition were proceeding. Trials had already begun in July of that year of a high velocity 105mm gun to fit the breech and mounting of the 20-pounder. This would enable Centurion to be upgraded at less cost than producing a new vehicle.

A sense of urgency was added to the trials, when during the Hungarian uprising in November 1956 the designers had a unique opportunity to examine at first hand the enemy's capability. When a Soviet T54 that had been captured by the Hungarian patriots was driven into the grounds of the British Embassy, unfortunately diplomatic niceties prevailed and the Embassy intelligence staff had but a brief chance to examine the vehicle when it was measured and photographed before being returned. During this frenzied activity the armour plate was erroneously measured as 120mm at 60 degrees when it is really 100mm at 54 degrees.

As result of this investigation the new gun was required to be able to defeat this amount of armour and trials were held with the 20-pounder, 105mm and the L1A1 120mm of Conqueror. The 105mm easily exceeded the requirement with a 25 per cent increase in power over the 20-pounder. User trials took place at range 7B Hohne beginning on 15 July 1959 and were carried out by crews from the 4th\7th Royal Dragoon Guards, using two vehicles converted by 7th Armoured Workshops. The 105mm was extensively tested and after this the gun was enthusiastically accepted into service.

Also at about this time the 3rd Dragoon Guards and 4th/7th Royal Dragoon Guards with Mk VIII Centurions had conducted time trials. In November of that year a Mk VIII Centurion was fitted with additional armour plate on the glacis in the shape of a 2in (50mm) patch welded on, by doing this the protection then was raised to 5in (126mm) which was proof against the 100mm APHE round used by the T54. This up-armouring was then applied to most Centurion gun tanks in British service.

The combination of a glacis plate that was proof against the T54 100mm gun and a new gun that could destroy the T54 at long range was the catalyst that was to spell the end for the requirement for a long-range tank killer, for such was the power of the 105mm that it was able to defeat any of the targets for the foreseeable future that Conqueror had been designed to destroy.

It was therefore decided in 1966 to withdraw Conqueror from active service. No other role was to be allocated for the vehicles; neither were the hulls to be used as the basis for specialist vehicles. This was the War Office's way of removing what in their eyes was a great drain on valuable resources, so therefore the only role remaining for the redundant vehicles was ignominy on the ranges as hard targets. This procedure was carried out with almost indecent haste, akin to the Labour government's destruction of the world-beating TSR2 later on. According to the records for the period it was all over by the middle of 1967.

The vehicles were discarded in a manner that can best be described as casual and not how one would have believed the British Army removes its old vehicles. Major Beaver of 13\18th Hussars remembers, 'that we just mounted up in the tanks drove them out to the ranges at Sennelager, parked where we were told then switched off and got back into trucks and returned to camp.' In the evening the REME went out to the area and started to remove anything that was of use to them in keeping Centurion on the road, and after that they were just abandoned in mostly working order. This method is still employed – as recently as 1996–97 Centurion ARVs were simply driven onto the ranges and left to be battered to scrap.

The optics were meant to be removed or destroyed, but from by own research and wanderings around derelict vehicles this did not always happen. Usually the easily removable optics, like driver's sights, were the ones removed with the rest staying where they were. During my many miles trekking around various ranges in the UK and BAOR I have been amazed at the condition of some of the optics. In one particular vehicle I climbed into the FCT and to my amazement the rangefinder moved as smoothly in its mount now as it would have nearly thirty years ago, so much so that apart from fogging on the lens I was actually able to take a range and read it as clear as if I had been on the range using it (but sadly the vehicle has since been vandalized). G. T. Smith recalls being on Warcop ranges and looking at the Conquerors there and finding them in good condition. In fact, his regiment (1RTR) managed to recover one and bring it back to Catterick where it was started up and eventually ended up on a plinth outside the barracks, although it did not remain there for long and its whereabouts is now unknown. Tpr Graham Stocks of 3 Dragoon Guards (Carabiniers) remembers that as his regiment was the last to possess Conqueror it was decided to use Lothian barracks in Detmold, West Germany, as a holding area for the remaining Conquerors in BAOR. So for a very short time a single Conqueror regiment existed, if only by dint of being in one location at the same time. This was just the sort of set-up in which many said that Conqueror should have been deployed, instead of in such a piecemeal manner. In the end, there was a final parade, which must surely have been awe-inspiring and I am still trying to track down any pictures of that day. The Conquerors were then removed for their final destinations in BAOR or the UK.

That then should really have been the end of the Conqueror story and for the large majority of the gun tanks it really was the end of the line, but for others, including some of the gun tanks, there was a second career in the offing. Although most of the gun tanks were by now relegated to the role of hard targets (we shall look at the survivors later), some of the ARVs, especially the Mk IIs soldiered on for some years yet. One of the main reasons was that

The end came quick and most Conquerors found themselves in compounds like this one at Sennelager. Note the abandoned air that the vehicles seem to give out and the front idler and some of the track missing from the vehicle nearest to the camera. Tank Museum.

they remained, until the introduction of the Challenger ARV, the most powerful ARV in the world. I can well remember during my early days in training in the Army that a Conqueror ARV would come round the road at what seemed to be a great speed by the JLR RAC. It almost always seemed at about 1600 hours every day and always attached behind it rattling and rolling and looking very forlorn would be one of the first Chieftains.

They were also of great value to MVEE during the time that the Shir I tank that was developed from Chieftain was being produced for Iran and which would later form the basis for Challenger I. At that time the Army had absolutely nothing else with the pulling and winching power capable of recovering dead Shirs across country. If a Centurion ARV was

used to try to move a Shir, it usually ended up with the Centurion winching itself towards the dead Shir.

The Centurion ARVs slowly but surely replaced even ARVs until it seemed that none would survive. And this would not take too long, for as we have seen there were only twenty-eight Conquerors built, eight Mk Is and twenty Mk IIs. The only two hulls that can still be recognized as Mk Is are on Warcop ranges and Salisbury plain. At the time of writing I know of no fully restored Mk I ARV. The Mk IIs are rather better represented; recognizable hulls exist, with one on Otterburn training area which may soon be recovered and possibly fully restored – let's hope so! There is another at Bordon with the REME where it is used as a training aid for recovery crews, with most of its time spent sitting in a water-filled hole on the area and every so often it is winched out and then pushed back in. It is in good company, however, as sitting in the next hole is a Conqueror gun tank, 41 BA 27. If this makes it seem that the REME at Bordon are heartless, then the next story will change that.

Pride of place in the REME historic vehicle collection is a fully restored to running order Mk II ARV. In the late seventies 01 BB 78 was recovered from the ranges and after a lot of work repairing it (often manufacturing spares as none were remaining) it was brought to the standard that one can see today. This vehicle really is a credit to the museum and those who restored her, well worth the trip to the museum just to see it. If you are lucky, you may even see it on a day when it is running.

The next ARV that we look at surely must bear a charmed life – 04 CC 76 was allocated to the Proof Establishment at Shoeburyness on 7 December 1965, where it worked hard. But time and lack of readily available spares took its toll and although it was still drivable it would not perform under load, hardly a good advert for an ARV. There were those in authority, thinking only of the financial side, who felt that the best thing would be to sell it to the MoD as a hard target and have done with it. However, the vehicle was saved and transferred to the Imperial War Museum at Duxford, where in the vehicle wing we have probably the most knowledgeable team on restoring life to dead Conquerors that can be found anywhere in the world today. It has found a good home and will in the fullness of time be fully restored to running order and fitted with all its associated equipment just as in its glory days. The fact that it can be driven at all I can amply testify to by having been privileged to ride on it in August

A Mk II ARV used as a recovery training aid by the REME at Bordon; this vehicle is now owned by Mr D. Arnold and is to be fully restored.

Also at Bordon the REME historic vehicle collection's fully working museum exhibit. Author.

1992 during the Military Day at Duxford, where it performed well although at times it was a struggle. However, if the number of video and still cameras that were pointed at it as we drove by were anything to go by, this will be a favourite for years to come.

The best place to start our look at the surviving gun tanks must be at the Tank Museum at Bovington, and we shall start with the one that Mike Norman lists as the 'only surviving one in good condition'. We are very lucky for at Bovington besides the 'only surviving' Conqueror, the museum also boasts three more. Let's then start with the Tank Museum's vehicle, 40 BA 86, a Mk I in service from 18 March 1955 before finally

A Mk II ARV pictured whilst serving with the Proof Establishment at Shoeburyness. P&EE.

coming to settle in the Tank Museum. The vehicle can in fact still be driven, but this now only happens when there is a requirement to move vehicles around the museum. Today the vehicles are more likely to be dragged around than driven, due to the cost of getting fuel into the vehicle, then making good any damage that occurs to it and finally having to drain the fuel out. It would be nice to see this Conqueror up and running on one of the summer Tank Days held at the museum.

Just across the road, acting as a gateguard for what used to be the Junior Leaders Regiment Royal Armoured Corps but now used as barracks for the permanent staff at Bovington camp, is 40 BA 95, a Mk II in service from 20 June 1955 until its eventual arrival at the JLR. This was one of the original troop trials vehicles and also it was the first production Mk II. Unusually, it has only had half of the machined rim to the bottom of the turret that was such a distinctive feature, but I can find no reason for this omission. It was actually driven into place by S/Sgt John Doughty of 3 RTR, and by one of those great military coincidences he was one of the instructors who laboured so hard to teach very young boys including the author, the rudiments of 20-pounder and 105mm Centurion gunnery all those years ago.

The final vehicle that can be recognized as a Conqueror is 05 BB 96, mounted on a plinth outside

This is the first Mk II Conqueror and can be seen today by visitors to the Tank Museum, as it is the gate guard for Stanley Barracks just across the road from the museum. If you look closely at the picture you will notice that the machining on the bottom of the turret only goes halfway round instead of all the way. No explanation can be found for this anomaly. Author.

the WOs' and Sgts' mess. This is another Mk II in service from 21 May 1959 until it was struck off on 22 June 1964. It is in fairly good condition and as the mood takes Bovington Garrison it is repainted, although really it should be in a building protected from the elements.

Before leaving Bovington we must mention the other Conqueror that is located there. This is also at the Tank Museum and as we have already seen it is

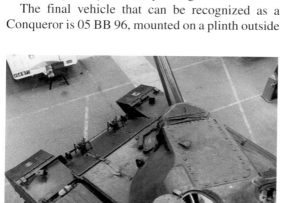

A shot of the Mk I that survives in the Tank Museum at Bovington. Author.

The general public does not often see this Mk II as it sits outside the entrance to the Warrant Officers' and Sergeant's mess at Bovington. It is lucky in that every so often the garrison gives it a new coat of paint. Author.

the gas-turbine test bed, 07 BA 70. After it had completed its turbine trials it was used in a variety of trials until it was converted into a dynamometer vehicle and based at Christchurch in Hampshire. When I visited it, the vehicle had been fitted with Chieftain track and sprockets, the rear suspension arms were welded in the up position, and it was fitted with a large enclosed box-like cab and a diesel engine. On finishing its service at Christchurch it ended up at the Tank Museum, where it was driven onto a ramp overlooking the old running track, and used as a commentary box. In its present form it retains the box structure that was fitted at Christchurch but if you look at it carefully you can see its Conqueror lineage, and one can only hope that it and the surviving gas-turbine engine can be reunited and displayed as such.

The next major source for surviving Conquerors is the outstation of the Imperial War Museum at Duxford in Cambridge. As well as a large collection of aircraft, the museum also boasts a military vehicle wing and working within that wing a small team of AFV enthusiasts have become experts at restoring Conquerors and many other AFVs to running condition. Led by Andy Hutchenson they have produced immaculately restored vehicles from hulks brought in from ranges in the UK.

They have three Conquerors that are runners and regularly appear in the Military Days at Duxford.

The driving cab of 07 BA 70, slightly more luxurious than in its early days. Author.

One of the vehicles we have already met is the Mk II ARV from Shoeburyness, but the two remaining vehicles are of interest. The first that we shall look at is 40 BA 81; this vehicle is unusual in that instead of the familiar turret of Conqueror it is fitted with what is known as a Windsor turret. This is simply a circular weight fitted to the turret ring and is used to enable trials to be carried out simulating either the weight of a turret not yet produced or of a vehicle increase in weight due to possibly up-armouring or similar.

This vehicle is a Mk I and came into service on 18 March 1955 and served until 22 October 1975. It was one of the original twenty vehicles sent to

07 BA 70 in its bright yellow paint scheme while working as a dynamometer vehicle at Christchurch. Author.

Showing the new Rolls Royce engine in the dynamometer vehicle, a far cry from its days with the gas turbine. Author.

07 BA 70 in its present role as a commentary box at the Tank Museum. Author.

BAOR on the troop trial and then was used at FVRDE before arriving at the D and M school at Bovington, whereupon it soon lost its Conqueror turret and was fitted with the Windsor turret. It arrived there in the tender care of Lt. Col. John Gillman, a well known AFV enthusiast, becoming the property of the Tank Museum, but the Museum had nowhere to exhibit it or for that matter store it. It was decided to long-loan it to Duxford, where

after many problems they managed to get it running. It is now waiting time and space for a full restoration project to be carried out on it. It is an interesting survivor in its present configuration, as apart from minor differences it resembles closely what the Caernarvon would have looked like. It can be used to compare the two, as a picture of Caernarvon 07 BA 77 fitted with a *Windsor* turret often appears in books. It is hoped that when it is

A sight that many thought they would not see again – three Conquerors all being worked on. The centre one belongs to Duxford, while the one on the right was being made ready to be exchanged with Russia for a JS2, and the left-hand one was to be the gate guard for Castlemartin. A. Hutchenson.

fully restored the team is going to fit a surplus Centurion III turret to it and thus create the nearest that we will have to a Caernarvon. This will be of great interest, as no Caernarvon*s* have survived in their original build.

Duxford's other Conqueror is 05 BB 94, a Mk II in service from 21 January 1959 until 10 September 1967, when it was struck off and presented to the Imperial War Museum as a gift. Due to the love and care lavished on it by the vehicle wing team it also is still in running condition and can enable the public on open days to see and hear the sound of Conqueror's Meteor engine in full blast as it traverses the display circuit. It also managed to appear in one of the stunts arranged by television star Jeremy Beadle, when it was shown crushing what the unsuspecting victims thought was a member of staff's car at Duxford.

The biggest restoration job that the team at Duxford has undertaken was the rebuild of 05 BB 92. This was Mk II in service from 21 May 1959 until 29 December 1966, during which time it managed to appear in the now defunct Daily Sketch newspaper on 18 May 1957 whilst serving with the 17\21st Lancers. The occasion was the bicentenary of the regiment and presentation of a new Guidon. The vehicle was pictured with two young lance orderlies, twenty-year-old Tpr Raymond Holmes and eighteen-year-old Tpr Charles Bugg, in full dress uniform in front of it; the picture was also used by Profile Publications to illustrate their profile on the Conqueror. Once it had been struck from strength it was consigned to the ranges at Colchester from which it was recovered and restored to its former glory by the Duxford team. In one of those strange twists of fate it was eventually exchanged for a Josef Stalin II with the Russian Tank Museum, thus giving Duxford the only one in the Western world. It is curious to think that it now rests in a museum in a country in which not so long ago Conqueror may have been called on to destroy the successors to the JS2.

At the same time that the Duxford team recovered 05 BB 92 they also recovered 04 BA 22. This was restored to a non-running gate guard and

now sits outside the RAC ranges at Castlemartin. The original gate guard, 41 BA 03, was a Mk II in service from 1 November 1955 to 23 September 1965 and has now been removed for restoration in Kent and it is hoped that it will eventually be on display again one day.

We have briefly mentioned 41 BA 27, the gun tank at Bordon. This is a Mk II and was in service from 31 July 1958 and was finally struck off in July 1965. It is now used as a recovery aid by the REME. It is located in a hollow depression in the ground, which very quickly fills up with water. The recovery crews under training will come to it and work out how best to recover it, then winch it from its watery home, be debriefed on what went right and wrong, then it is simply pushed back into its hole ready for another day. The day that I went to photograph it I was privileged to have it specially recovered for me, all of which was unexpected and made for good video archive material.

A major user of Conqueror*s* was the Proof and Experimental Establishment at Shoeburyness. In addition to the ARV, which we have already covered, they used four gun tanks. These were modified in various forms to enable them to carry out the specialist role that was envisaged for them. This was mostly as a mobile base for mounting experimental weapons. Due to their great weight they were able to provide stable platforms for the weapon mountings. This saved money, as otherwise special concrete bases would have had to be built each time.

40 BA 10 started life as a Mk II in service from 27 February 1956 to 16 March 1966 and 41 BA 11 was another Mk II, in service from 9 March 1956 to 8 June 1977. Both vehicles had their turrets removed, large metal floors covered the whole of the fighting compartment, and a driver's cab was added which protruded beyond the front idler wheels. This was added as the area covered by some of the weapons mounted over the old fighting compartment meant that access to the driver's cab would have proved difficult. Modified into this role they have given sterling service as mounts for many experimental weapons. 41 BA 68, a Mk II in service

The Imperial War Museum's Conqueror at Duxford. Just after this the author was invited to have a drive and it promptly broke down! Author.

05 BB 92 during its working day poses with two lance orderlies from the 17th/21st Lancers for a picture that appeared in the now defunct Daily Sketch. *Tank Museum.*

05 BB 92 pictured in September 1986 at Duxford looking rather sorry for itself. It had just been recovered from the ranges and was awaiting refurbishment ready to exchange with Russia for a JS2. A. Hutchenson.

05 BB 92 looking much happier, although it is ironic that the country whose vehicles it was designed to destroy now provides it with a home. Of interest are the Centurion and Chieftain either side that were 'acquired' by the Russians. B. Fleming.

41 BA 22 after undergoing restoration, now serving as a gate guard for the RAC ranges at Castlemartin in Wales. Author.

41 BA 03, the original gate guard at Castlemartin being removed prior to being replaced by 41 BA 22. It is now in the south of England awaiting restoration itself. A. Hutchenson.

41 BA 22 after being dragged in from the ranges. Compare this to the picture of it serving as Castlemartin gate guard. A. Hutchenson.

41 BA 27 being used as a recovery aid by the REME at Bordon. It has been bought by a diving company to sink as a diver's training aid, but attempts are being made to buy it back for restoration. One can only hope! Author.

from 31 May 1958 to 8 June 1971 was also converted in the same manner, but was the last to stop being powered by its own engine on 21 March 1990. The other two were just towed into the position required of them and left until it was time to be moved to a new location. The final vehicle is 41 BA 39, Mk II in service from 18 March 1958 to 17 January 1967. This has had the barrel removed and the turret gutted. A large-angle iron target-carrying frame was welded to the top of the turret and in this mode it is towed behind another vehicle as a target carrier.

Lieutenant Gilruth, who later became Deputy Commander RAC Centre and Bovington Camp, retained fond memories of his Conqueror troop. When I showed him the pictures of the vehicle in its current condition, he remarked, 'just think of all the work I used to do on the Conqueror in the troop and now look at it.'

Our next vehicle is 07 BA 75; this is a reworked Caernarvon to Mk II standards. Mr D. Arnold, another well known name in vehicle and aircraft restoration, once owned the vehicle, but it is now believed to be in the United States. Before export, the vehicle was in very good condition and was also a runner, and was probably the most complete Conqueror surviving anywhere. Originally part of the collection of vehicles at the Royal College of Military Science at Shrivenham, it now enjoys a life away from being a museum piece. This is an interesting survivor because it is the best surviving example of a rebuilt Caernarvon (two others do exist, but they are on Kirkcudbright ranges). It also is one of the vehicles that were taken on the Middle East trials by the 14\20th Hussars all those years ago.

Out of all our survivors the prize for the most unusual must go to a vehicle that at one time was part of the Budge Collection. Although it is numbered 02 BB 09, it is in fact a combination of two vehicles. Mr C. Evans bought the remains of 02 BB 09 and 40 BA 92 from Shoeburyness and using bits from each 02 BB 92 was reborn. Amongst the jobs that had to be done to make it look like a Conqueror again was the replacement of the driver's hatch and surrounding roof area as this had been flame cut out during its days at Shoeburyness. It is as fine a piece of welding as you could wish for – when you are in the driver's cab, unless you knew that this was not the original roof, you would never be able to tell and certainly not from the outside. One other strange feature is the engine decks, in that they are no longer in one piece, having been cut in half, again a legacy of its days at Shoeburyness.

What a crew! A very heavily modified 41 BA 10 from Shoeburyness. Notice the driver's cab extension to the right of the picture. The weapon is a 4.5 in naval gun. Tim Royall.

The one-time vehicle of Brigadier P. A. M. Gilruth of the 4/7 RDG, looking slightly different to when he knew it. The large frame fitted to the turret was to carry a target. Author.

41 BA 10 showing more clearly how drastic the conversion was. By now it had ceased to move under its own power so the driver's cab extension has been removed. Author.

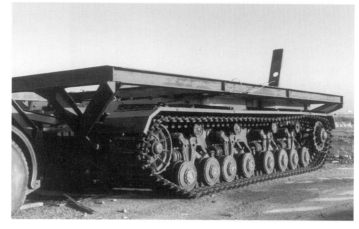

41 BA 11 converted into a similar mode as 41 BA 10. Author.

41 BA 11 in its previous existence as a gun tank before conversion at Shoeburyness. Tank Museum.

41 BA 68, recorded as the last working Conqueror in MoD service to move under its own power until its engine seized. Geoff Stobbard standing on the catwalk gives an idea of the size of this conversion. Author.

07 BA 75 pictured at the RMCS Shrivenham before being sold to a private owner and then sold again to an owner in the USA. Although the brass case in front is from Conqueror, the HESH round is from a Chieftain.

40 BA 92 with no turret prior to private purchase. B Fleming.

40 BA 92 showing the hole cut in the driver's cab area. B Fleming.

02 BB 09 arriving at the then Budge collection. This is two vehicles put together to make up the one good one. B Fleming.

40 BA 92 looking slightly better with its turret back in place. B Fleming.

02 BB 09 in location at the AF Budge military vehicle collection before being sold and exported to the USA. Note the use of a Chieftain HESH round again on the front wing. Author.

The decks were cut to allow easy access when an experimental mount was fitted. One such mount was the turret for the SP 70 self-propelled gun, which nearly made it into the British Army as the new SP, only to fall victim to cuts with no new SP appearing until the purchase of AS 90. So although this is a mixture of vehicles it is important in that it is one more survivor and a runner at that. 40 BA 92 was not so lucky and is now residing to the east of Imber village on Salisbury plain with the turret from another Conqueror leaning against it.

Although not strictly complete survivors, I feel it is worth mentioning the two vehicles at Kirkcudbright in Scotland, as they are important in that they are both ex-Caernarvons. One vehicle, which was 07 BA 72, has been used at some time in mine trials but looks in fairly good condition considering. The gun has been removed and the hole plated up, and all catwalks are missing along with the bins. No.2 suspension unit is also gone on the left side, but at the end of the day yet another Caernarvon is reasonably intact. The second vehicle, 07 BA 74, is actually on the range but does not look as if it has been engaged for a long time. Again the gun is missing, as are catwalks and bins, but the left side suspension is intact and it has a good condition track fitted. The right side track has split and has curled up forward of the vehicle.

Another Conqueror that seems as though it may well be crossing the Atlantic is 41 BA 16. This vehicle was formerly one of the collection of gate guard vehicles at the vehicle depot Ludgershall. When that depot closed down as part of defence cuts the vehicle was purchased by Pounds scrapyard of Portsmouth. When I last saw it, a large amount of ship's anchor chain had been placed on

07 BA 72, one of the rebuilt Caernarvons now in use at Kirkcudbright ranges, possibly for use in mine trials. Kirkcudbright ranges.

Another Kirkcudbright vehicle, this time it is 07 BA 74 taken in May 1992. It is another of the rebuilt Caernarvons. Kirkcudbright ranges.

top of the turret to prevent access to vandals. On enquiring as to its ultimate fate I was told that an American was interested in it, although no matter what the owner of the yard would not let it be cut up for scrap. During its service life it served mostly at FVRDE and took part in trials in trying to lower the infrared signature from the exhaust pipes, and if you look closely at the picture you will not see the large round exhaust pipes on the vehicle.

The next vehicle we look at is 40 BA 98; this is located outside the Belgium Tank Museum in Brussels. I have a particular interest in this vehicle as at the time that I was carrying out my research for this book I was contacted by the museum to see if I could discover anything, including the vehicle registration of their Conqueror. This vehicle had an

interesting career and is in fact a tank that we have met already. It came into service on 20 June 1955 and was struck off on 9 August 1967. It was an original troop trial vehicle and was one of two also to carry the experimental lightweight fire-control turret. For the troop trial it had been issued to the 4/7 Royal Dragoon Guards, during which time it was in collision with 40 BA 96. By taking parts from 40 BA 96 the vehicle was repaired and finished the trial. On being reissued it served in BAOR until it was withdrawn. It was designated as a hard target and at some time in its life it became the property of the West German *Bundesamt für Wehrtechnik und Beschaffung*. From there, it was transported by the British Army to Brussels and to the Tank Museum. In correspondence with the

William the Conqueror stood for many years acting as gate guard for the MoD vehicle depot at Ludgershall. When that depot was closed the vehicle ended up in Pounds scrapyard but I am assured that it will not be sold for scrap; more than likely it also will join the other Conquerors in the USA. Author.

This is 40 BA 98, that at the time of writing sits outside at the Belgium Tank Museum. This is one of the original trial vehicles and also was fitted with the lightweight FCT. Belgium Tank Museum.

Museum they tell me that the vehicle has two armour-piercing penetrations on the turret and machine gun impacts on the mudguards, in poor status. This is another vehicle that could well do with being indoors and restored. It will be interesting to visit one day and discover whether it was issued with the lightweight FCT or whether that was removed and a conventional one fitted.

The final Conqueror that I wish to look at is 40 BA 90. This vehicle is located at the French Armour School at Samur. It is a Mk I vehicle built at Dalmuir and issued on 25 April 1955. It was withdrawn from service on 21 May 1968 and was presented to the French Armour School. The staff at the museum say that the vehicle is in very good condition and could be made a runner, but would

need new final drives. These are not easily available and the cost involved will mean that we will probably never see this vehicle moving again under its own power.

This ends our look at surviving vehicles, and whilst I accept that there are several Conquerors in fairly good condition on many ranges, I have dealt mostly with those that are accessible to the general public, even if Moscow is rather a long way to go to see a Conqueror. The list that appears in Chapter 9 will show the location and fate of most Conquerors. Whilst I have tried to find as many vehicles as possible time has taken its toll, with many being destroyed beyond recognition. Indeed, I must confess in the past to having sent some of those vehicles to that great scrapyard in the sky. Just by

40 BA 90 is pictured in the French Cavalry Museum at Samur. With a lot of work it is said that this vehicle could run again, although that is highly unlikely.

finding some part of the vehicle I have managed to piece together its registration number and sometimes its history. In Germany that is very hard to achieve now, as the 'green policy' on the ranges means that once a hard target has been reduced to a certain level it must be removed for scrap, so those that I can remember as being on particular ranges have now long gone.

So here we are at the end of the Conqueror story, although we traced its beginning way back to the dark days of World War II and all the trials and problems that trying to bring such a radical new vehicle into service caused. Then there were all the cancellations and the creation of the FV214 which made it into service and shone briefly before it was replaced. The armour battle carried on with Centurion and Chieftain, with both now relegated to the role of hard targets. I have tried to let the

story of Conqueror unfold itself, whether it would have been able to carry out its role or whether it was just a waste of time, whether it was loved by the crews or hated. I feel that it is too easily dismissed by AFV authors in just a few lines, usually consisting of 'Conqueror, was big noisy and disliked by all who served in it.' I believe that is a negative way of looking at it, and the point of the vehicle being produced for one role, and one role only, is always totally missed. I think that those who predicted its demise before it was even built might well be surprised at just how popular the Conqueror is today. We can go and see it either static or running at Duxford, and several models have been recently produced of Conqueror and the Mk II ARV. I have built a 1/8th scale working model of Conqueror and every time I take it on show I can guarantee that someone will come up to me and say

'I was on Conqueror', and then tell me all about their experiences. The Conqueror story is important as it filled a gap, albeit for a short time, in the British armoured inventory, and although it will never be as famous as the Tiger or Sherman I believe it deserves its place in the history of armoured fighting vehicles.

Appendix 1: History and Disposal of the Conqueror

In this Chapter, I have listed all known Conquerors and have shown, where possible, their date into service and out of service and, where known, their ultimate fate. It will become apparent during reading that a great many of the vehicles were taken out of service at the same time, and where a not known is shown it means just that, that no hard evidence was available but no guesses were made. This information is based on official MoD records, my own research around ranges and training areas and War Office documents in the Public Records office. I would be very foolish if I was to state that this is 100 per cent accurate, but it is the best with the available information. Grey areas include those vehicles that are or might be going to the USA – have they actually left the UK? If you know, please let me know!

Conqueror in Service, History and Disposal					
VRN	**Mk**	**ROF**	**In Service**	**Disposal**	**History**
40 BA 75	I	Leeds	31/03/54	Not known	First true Conqueror
40 BA 76	I	Leeds	22/08/54	12/08/70	Converted to scrap
40 BA 77	I	Leeds	23/06/55	Not known	Hard target
40 BA 78	I	Leeds	24/05/55	23/03/65	Not known
40 BA 79	I	Leeds	06/10/54	18/07/66	Hard target
40 BA 80	I	Dalmuir	24/05/55	22/10/75	Once issued to 4th/7th Royal Dragoon Guards
40 BA 81	I	Dalmuir	18/03/55	22/10/75	Troop trial vehicle, now Duxford with Windsor turret
40 BA 82	I	Dalmuir	18/03/55	Not known	Troop trial vehicle
40 BA 83	I	Dalmuir	18/03/55	Not known	Troop trial vehicle
40 BA 84	I	Dalmuir	25/04/55	23/05/59	Troop trial vehicle, then to Shoeburyness range, scrap by 02/07/65
40 BA 85	I	Dalmuir	18/03/55	Not known	Troop trial vehicle
40 BA 86	I	Dalmuir	18/03/55	27/06/61	Now exhibit at Tank Museum, Bovington
40 BA 87	I	Dalmuir	25/04/55	27/09/67	Converted to training aid, possibly D&M School
40 BA 88	I	Dalmuir	24/05/55	Not known	Possibly used as a training aid

This shows three Conquerors on the anti-tank range at Haltern in Germany. When the picture was taken they did not appear to have been fired at for some time. Note the American M47 in the background. The vehicles are 02 BB 25 left, 41 BA 50 centre, 41 BA 61 right. Author.

40 BA 92 on Salisbury Plain with the turret from another Conqueror leaning against it. Author.

The turrets of 40 BA 85 and 41 BA 15 on the anti-tank range Sennybridge. In the background can be seen the hulls of two Mk V Ferrets. Author.

40 BA 89	I	Dalmuir	25/04/55	03/08/67	Hard target
40 BA 90	I	Dalmuir	25/05/55	21/05/68	Hard target, then to French Tank Museum at Samur
40 BA 91	I	Dalmuir	25/05/55	29/12/68	Hard target on Thetford training area
40 BA 92	I	Dalmuir	24/05/55	04/02/86	Shoeburyness, then Salisbury plain as a hard target
40 BA 93	I	Dalmuir	24/05/55	10/06/87	Troop trials vehicle
40 BA 94	I	Dalmuir	24/05/55	10/08/67	Hard target range 1A Hohne Germany
40 BA 95	II	Dalmuir	20/06/55	Not known	First Mk II. Now gate guard at Stanley Barracks
40 BA 96	II	Dalmuir	20/06/55	20/05/85	Troop trial vehicle issued to 4/7 DG, collision with 40 BA 98, cannibalized, then to Chertsey
40 BA 97	II	Dalmuir	20/06/55	15/07/65	Troop trial vehicle
40 BA 98	II	Dalmuir	20/06/55	09/08/67	Troop trial vehicle issued to 4/7DG, in collision with 40 BA 96, fitted with lightweight FCT, now in Belgium Tank Museum
40 BA 99	II	Dalmuir	20/06/55	04/03/68	Troop trial vehicle fitted with lightweight FCT
41 BA 00	II	Dalmuir	20/06/55	02/01/68	Hard target
41 BA 01	II	Dalmuir	14/09/55	17/08/67	Hard target
41 BA 02	II	Dalmuir	14/11/55	17/08/67	Hard target
41 BA 03	II	Dalmuir	01/11/55	23/09/65	Ex-Castlemartin gate guard, now awaiting restoration
41 BA04	II	Dalmuir	03/11/55	Not known	Hard target
41 BA 05	II	Dalmuir	13/12/55	21/08/70	Mine trials vehicle
41 BA 06	II	Dalmuir	13/12/55	03/11/71	Not known
41 BA 07	II	Dalmuir	20/12/55	11/07/66	Hard target
41 BA 08	II	Dalmuir	19/03/56	11/07/66	Lulworth trials vehicle
41 BA 09	II	Dalmuir	22/12/56	16/06/67	Hard target Warcop ranges
41 BA 10	II	Dalmuir	27/02/56	16/03/56	Test bed at Shoeburyness
41 BA 11	II	Dalmuir	09/03/56	08/06/77	Test bed at Shoeburyness
41 BA 12	II	Dalmuir	09/03/56	21/09/65	Not known
41 BA 13	II	Dalmuir	09/04/56	09/08/66	Hard target
41 BA 14	II	Dalmuir	19/03/56	09/07/66	Hard target School of Infantry
41 BA 15	II	Dalmuir	25/06/56	18/08/59	Armament wing FVRDE
41 BA 16	II	Dalmuir	19/03/56	Not known	FVRDE test on lower IR signature from exhaust, then gate guard at Ludgershall, then to Pounds scrap yard for export to USA

02 BB 24 in a wintry setting on Sennelager ranges in Germany. WO2 Smith MBE, Sennelager range control.

A very gaudy 41 BA 34 on the RAF bombing ranges at Tain in Scotland. RAF Tain.

A turretless 40 BA 49 at the REME depot in Bordon. Author.

41 BA 17	II	Dalmuir	21/02/57	12/04/60	Hard target
41 BA 18	II	Dalmuir	01/05/58	July 65	Hard target
41 BA 19	II	Dalmuir	01/05/58	Not known	Hard target
41 BA 20	II	Dalmuir	05/05/58	July 65	Hard target
41 BA 21	II	Dalmuir	01/04/58	July 65	Hard target
41 BA 22	II	Dalmuir	20/08/53	01/04/58	Castlemartin replacement gateguard
41 BA 23	II	Dalmuir	05/05/58	03/08/67	Hard target
41 BA 24	II	Dalmuir	20/05/58	09/05/68	Hard target
41 BA 25	II	Dalmuir	05/05/58	July 65	Hard target
41 BA 26	II	Dalmuir	02/07/58	20/03/68	Training aid
41 BA 27	II	Dalmuir	31/07/58	July 65	REME Bordon
41 BA 28	II	Dalmuir	02/07/58	July 65	Hard target
41 BA 29	II	Dalmuir	01/05/58	July 65	Hard target
41 BA 30	II	Dalmuir	02/07/58	09/08/67	Hard target
41 BA 31	II	Dalmuir	25/07/58	20/09/66	Declared total wreck at Shoeburyness 29/07/80
41 BA 32	II	Dalmuir	02/07/58	18/04/69	Hard target
41 BA 33	II	Dalmuir	18/11/58	July 65	Not known
41 BA 34	II	Dalmuir	28/10/58	20/09/66	RAF bombing range Tain, Scotland
41 BA 35	II	Dalmuir	18/11/58	20/09/56	Hard target
41 BA 36	II	Dalmuir	03/05/58	06/10/64	RAC Centre vehicle, then Larkhill ranges 24/08/83
41 BA 37	II	Dalmuir	03/03/58	14/12/69	Hard target
41 BA 38	II	Dalmuir	18/11/58	July 65	Not known
41 BA 39	II	Dalmuir	18/03/58	17/01/67	Target carrier Shoeburyness
41 BA 40	II	Dalmuir	24/03/58	24/09/65	Not known
41 BA 41	II	Dalmuir	18/03/58	04/08/68	Not known
41 BA 42	II	Dalmuir	18/03/58	14/06/67	School of Infantry hard target
41 BA 43	II	Dalmuir	31/03/58	10/03/67	Hard target
41 BA 44	II	Dalmuir	18/03/58	09/08/67	Hard target
41 BA 45	II	Dalmuir	18/03/58	Not known	Not known
41 BA 46	II	Dalmuir	31/03/58	16/06/69	Hard target Warcop
41 BA 47	II	Dalmuir	01/04/58	10/03/67	Hard target Salisbury Plain
41 BA 48	II	Dalmuir	18/03/58	July 65	Not known
41 BA 49	II	Dalmuir	01/04/58	July 65	REME Bordon
41 BA 50	II	Dalmuir	18/03/58	July 65	Hard target, Haltern Germany
41 BA 51	II	Dalmuir	20/05/58	Not known	Hard target Pirbright ranges
41 BA 52	II	Dalmuir	20/08/58	19/04/68	Hard target
41 BA 53	II	Dalmuir	20/05/58	20/09/67	Delivered to Major Inkester at Otterburn, then used in BAC Swingfire film
41 BA 54	II	Dalmuir	05/05/58	July 65	Not known

An ex-film star, 41 BA 53, was filmed by BAE having a strike on it by a Swingfire anti-tank missile. This was shown on the Frederick Forsyth series on the British Army in the eighties. Author.

An unknown vehicle on Otterburn ranges showing the effects of HEAT round strikes. Author.

The very fragile remains of 41 BA 23 at the Castlemartin ranges. Author.

41 BA 55	II	Dalmuir	20/05/58	July 65	Not known
41 BA 56	II	Dalmuir	20/05/58	31/08/64	Not known
41 BA 57	II	Dalmuir	01/05/58	Not known	Not known
41 BA 58	II	Dalmuir	06/06/58	16/04/69	Not known
41 BA 59	II	Dalmuir	20/05/58	Not known	Hard target Salisbury Plain
41 BA 60	II	Dalmuir	07/10/58	Not known	Not known
41 BA 61	II	Dalmuir	02/07/58	03/06/67	Hard target Haltern, Germany
41 BA 62	II	Dalmuir	20/08/53	July 65	Not known
41 BA 63	II	Dalmuir	25/07/58	July 65	Not known
41 BA 64	II	Dalmuir	06/06/58	July 65	Not known
41 BA 65	II	Dalmuir	06/06/58	July 65	Not known
41 BA 66	II	Dalmuir	06/06/58	16/06/67	Hard target Warcop
41 BA 67	II	Dalmuir	06/06/58	July 65	Not known
41 BA 68	II	Dalmuir	03/10/58	08/06/71	Shoeburyness, last official runner engine seized 21/03/90
41 BA 69	II	Dalmuir	06/06/58	10/12/65	Not known
41 BA 70	II	Dalmuir	02/07/58	10/12/65	Not known
41 BA 71	II	Dalmuir	31/07/58	July 65	Not known
41 BA 72	II	Dalmuir	31/07/58	July 65	Not known
41 BA 73	II	Dalmuir	25/07/58	July 65	Not known
41 BA 74	II	Dalmuir	31/07/58	July 65	Not known
02 BB 09	II	Dalmuir	20/08/53	17/01/67	Budge collection, now suspected in USA
02 BB 10	II	Dalmuir	07/10/58	20/09/66	Shoeburyness, then sold as scrap August 79
02 BB 11	II	Dalmuir	14/08/58	16/06/67	Hard target Warcop
02 BB 12	II	Dalmuir	09/10/58	09/08/67	Hard target
02 BB 13	II	Dalmuir	14/08/58	July 65	Hard target
02 BB 14	II	Dalmuir	14/08/58	July 65	Hard target
02 BB15	II	Dalmuir	14/08/58	July 65	Hard target
02 BB 16	II	Dalmuir	14/08/58	July 65	Hard target
02 BB 17	II	Dalmuir	14/08/58	July 65	Hard target
02 BB 18	II	Dalmuir	09/10/58	09/08/67	Hard target
02 BB 19	II	Dalmuir	07/10/58	19/04/68	Hard target
02 BB 20	II	Dalmuir	14/10/58	Not known	Hard target Salisbury Plain
02 BB 21	II	Dalmuir	14/10/58	July 65	Hard target Battle run 9, Hohne, Germany
02 BB 22	II	Dalmuir	28/10/58	July 65	Hard target
02 BB 23	II	Dalmuir	14/10/58	July 65	Hard target
02 BB 24	II	Dalmuir	14/10/58	May 65	Hard target Belle Alliance range, Sennelager
02 BB 25	II	Dalmuir	14/10/58	July 65	Hard target Haltern, Germany
02 BB 26	II	Dalmuir	14/10/58	July 65	Hard target

41 BA 14 on Salisbury Plain. It has an unusual cover where the left headlight should be and perhaps this was going to be how the lights were to be mounted in later versions. Author.

A Mk I ARV with a Churchill turret placed on top, near the point-to-point course on Salisbury plain Author

02 BB 21 on Range 9 Hohne, Germany. When I found this vehicle even my Bundeswehr guides were surprised as they thought that all hulks like this had been cleared years ago. As can be seen, it has sprouted its own tree growing through the engine compartment. Author.

02 BB 27	II	Dalmuir	14/10/58	01/10/65	Hard target
02 BB 28	II	Dalmuir	28/10/58	July 65	Hard target
02 BB 29	II	Dalmuir	28/10/58	July 65	Hard target
02 BB 30	II	Dalmuir	28/10/58	09/08/67	Hard target
02 BB 31	II	Dalmuir	28/10/58	16/06/67	Hard target Warcop
02 BB 32	II	Dalmuir	18/11/58	May 65	Hard target
05 BB 78	II	Dalmuir	31/10/58	May 65	Not known
05 BB 79	II	Dalmuir	28/11/58	July 65	Not known
05 BB 80	II	Dalmuir	28/10/58	July 65	Not known
05 BB 81	II	Dalmuir	28/11/58	09/08/67	Hard target
05 BB 82	II	Dalmuir	28/11/58	July 65	Not known
05 BB 83	II	Dalmuir	28/11/58	02/12/74	Not known
05 BB 84	II	Dalmuir	04/12/58	May 65	Not known
05 BB 85	II	Dalmuir	04/12/58	16/06/67	Hard target Warcop
05 BB 86	II	Dalmuir	28/11/58	27/01/67	Hard target Tain, Scotland
05 BB 87	II	Dalmuir	04/12/58	May 65	Not known
05 BB 88	II	Dalmuir	04/12/58	09/08/67	Hard target
05 BB 89	II	Dalmuir	04/12/58	04/08/68	Not known
05 BB 90	II	Dalmuir	04/12/58	08/03/67	Not known
05 BB 91	II	Dalmuir	04/12/58	09/08/66	Hard target
05 BB 92	II	Dalmuir	02/01/59	29/12/66	Used as cover for Profile Publications *Conqueror* booklet with two 17/21st Lancers, then to ranges as hard target, recovered by Duxford and restored to full order. Now in Russian Tank Museum.
05 BB 93	II	Dalmuir	06/01/59	06/01/69	Hard target
05 BB 94	II	Dalmuir	02/01/59	10/09/67	Gift to Imperial War Museum at Duxford
05 BB 95	II	Dalmuir	21/05/59	Not known	Not known
05 BB 96	II	Dalmuir	21/05/59	22/06/64	Sgts' Mess, Bovington Camp
07 BB 92	II	Dalmuir	18/11/58	July 65	Not known
07 BB 93	II	Dalmuir	18/11/58	July 65	Not known
07 BB 94	II	Dalmuir	18/11/58	July 65	Not known
07 BB 95	II	Dalmuir	28/11/58	Not known	Not known

The following vehicle numbers were allocated under contract 6/FV16294. They would have been built as Mk IIs and also built at Dalmuir but it is highly unlikely that this contract was ever fulfilled. The numbers would have been 07 BB 97, 07 BB 98, 07 BB 99, 08 BB 00, 08 BB 01, 08 BB 02, 08 BB 03 and 08 BB 04.

The following vehicles were originally FV221 Caernarvons and were converted to FV214 Conqueror standards, and classified as Mk II/1/H. Externally, the hulls resembled a Mk I and the vehicle was the most modern Conqueror produced. 07 BA 68, 07 BA 71, 07 BA 72, 07 BA 74, 07 BA 75, 07 BA 76 and 07 BA 77. These were the last vehicles to be produced by ROF Dalmuir, after which the factory was eventually demolished and the land redeveloped.

This gives us a total number of 159 vehicles that served with the British Army but does not include prototypes. This number is made up as follows: five Mk I vehicles built at ROF Leeds, fifteen Mk I vehicles built at ROF Dalmuir and 132 Mk II vehicles also built at ROF Dalmuir. On top of this are the seven converted Caernarvons, giving a total of 159 vehicles. Twenty-eight ARVs were built, being eight Mk I and twenty Mk II vehicles.

The fate of other vehicles from the FV200 series is rather harder to determine, but the under mentioned vehicles were disposed of as shown in the table below.

It is not unusual for a civilian type registration number to be issued during the trial period.

This, then, is the end of the Conqueror story and I hope you agree that it has twisted and turned in its development and it must seem like a miracle that it ever saw the light of day. If you do ever get the chance to see one of the survivors in action, then please do so as it will leave you in awe of the power of this vehicle, if only from its sheer size.

Type	Reg No	Disposal
FV201 P1	JUU 689	Targetized
FV201 P3	KYW 13	Scrapped by T Ward Sheffield, 03/10/60
FV203 AVRE L	JXW 48	Cannibalized
FV201 DD	LYN 29	Destroyed at Lulworth
FV214 P1	N/A	Converted to hull only, then sold
FV214 P2	N/A	Converted to hull only, then sold
FV214 P3	N/A	Destroyed as target at Kirkcudbright
FV214 P5	N/A	Disposed of at Pendine ranges
FV214 P7	07 BA 70	Ex-gas turbine, now at Tank Museum

Appendix 2: Ammunition Details

Conqueror carried two types of 120mm round, if we discount the early issue of HE (High Explosive). Both of these rounds were designed for only one thing – the destruction of enemy armour.

The first that we shall examine is the APDS round. APDS stands for Armour Piercing Discarding Sabot. Then, as now, this is the main tank killing round. It is what is known as a kinetic energy round in that it achieves its destructive power from the speed with which it impacts the target. The actual projectile consists of two main parts – the inner core, which was made of tungsten, and the outer sheath. The reason for this layout is that to make the tungsten core travel fast enough to penetrate the armour it has to travel at high speed. To do this it needs to be aerodynamic and narrow in section; however, if it was to be loaded like this into the barrel it would not work with the projectile, having a diameter of approx. 50mm and the barrel of 120mm. That is where the outer sheath comes in. It is this part that is the actual sabot (or shoe). The core is encased in the sabot, which is held together by nylon driving bands and a thin wall of metal at the top of the round. The round weighs 21lb in its complete configuration before firing.

On firing, the round is pushed up the chamber, the nylon driving bands cut into the rifling, thus imparting spin to the projectile. This helps to stabilize the round in flight (today, most armour-piercing rounds are fin-stabilized). On leaving the barrel the air pressure forces the top of the round to split apart and break away. These were the parts held by the thin wall and are known as petals; at the same time the main sabot falls away to the rear leaving the inner core to travel to its target. The sabot can be dangerous to any troops in the open as it is travelling fast and out of control. The core carries on its flight, and due to its speed – in excess of 1,000m per second – its trajectory is very flat. In the base is a tracer element to help both gunner and commander track it.

On hitting the target a swivel tip on the front of the projectile will hit the armour and try to tip the round so that it can penetrate at a 90-degree angle, thus defeating the sloped armour. Once the round has started to penetrate it will punch its way through the metal. The wall will glow red hot and if it succeeds in defeating the armour it will then fly around the inside of the vehicle. Also following behind will be hot molten metal from the effect of penetration; all this combines to destroy anything in its path. Sometimes the tank gets lucky and there are many pictures showing vehicles surviving hits from AP rounds, notably Centurion in the Arab–Israeli wars and Chieftain in the Iran–Iraq conflict.

The AP round is the preferred tank killer as because of its flat trajectory it is usually far more accurate than other rounds.

The next anti-tank round is the HESH round. The High Explosive Squash Head belongs to the chemical rounds; another round in this group is the HEAT round. HESH is a much larger round and very much heavier. On firing, it has more of a curving trajectory than APDS, it also travels much slower, in the region of 650m per second. The round is 35lb in weight and consists of a shell that has a thick wall at the base of the round, thinning out until it reaches the tip of the round. The shell is filled with a plastic-type explosive and the fuse is situated in the base, along with the tracer elements.

On firing, the round travels down range in a lazy sort of arc. If it hits the target it will collapse on itself, hence the thin wall at the top. It forms a sort of cowpat on the armour, then the fuse hits and detonates the explosive, setting off an explosion that creates shockwaves that travel throughout the armour. These shockwaves break off large chunks of armour, known as scabs, on the inside of the vehicle and these are sent flying around inside, causing massive damage to personnel and equipment. Often from the outside the only indication that a vehicle has been hit by HESH is a

small indentation where the round hit – it is only inside that the damage becomes apparent.

The disadvantage of HESH is that it has a slow time of flight so the chance of it missing is increased and it can be defeated by spaced armour like bazooka plate or even a stowage bin. The advantage is that fire can be corrected on it by the gunner applying laid-down corrections; it can also be used in the High Explosive role with a lethality in the area of 50–70m.

There are other rounds that a tank could carry, but these were the only two that Conqueror carried.

120mm brass case sectioned with no propellant inside but showing the long primer; it was designed this length to ensure even burn of the propellant.

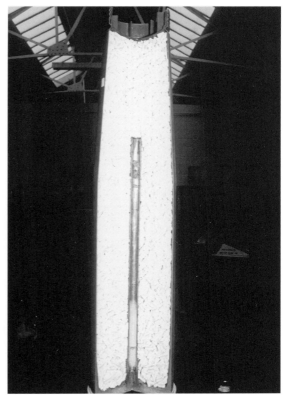

Fully sectioned 120mm brass case showing the propellant around the primer igniter.

Appendix 3: Technical Diagrams

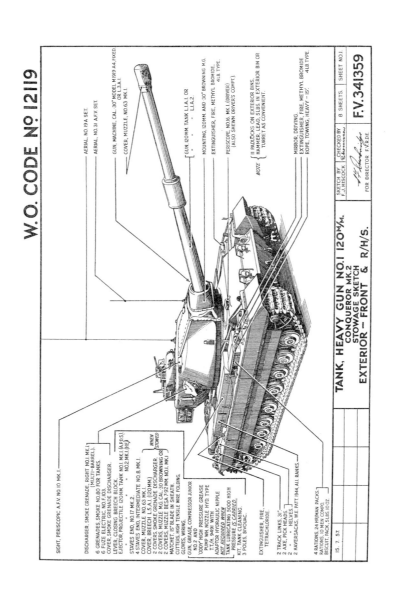

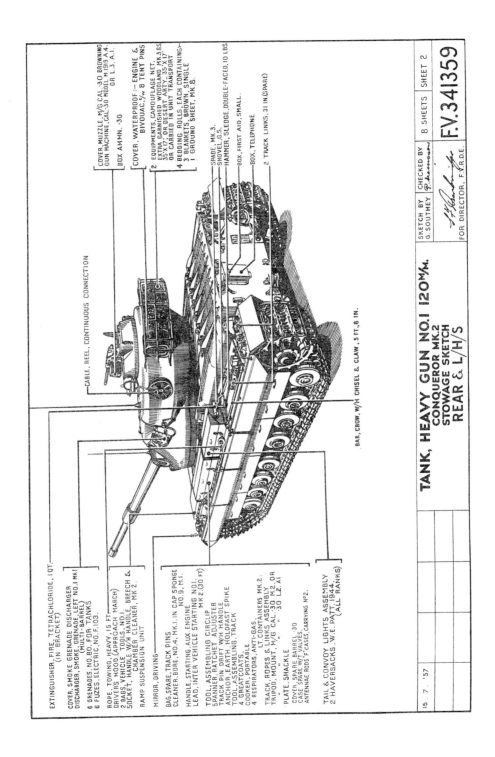

EXTINGUISHER, FIRE, TETRACHLORIDE, I QT.
(IN BRACKET)

COVER, SMOKE GRENADE DISCHARGER
DISCHARGER, SMOKE, GRENADE, LEFT NO.1 MK1
(MULTI-BARREL)
6 GRENADES, NO.80, FOR TANKS
6 FUZES, ELECTRIC, NO.F.103.

ROPE, TOWING, HEAVY, 15 FT.
DRIVER'S HOOD (APPROACH MARCH)
2 BAGS, VEHICLE TOOLS, NO.I
SOCKET, HANDLE W/H HANDLE, BREECH &
CHAMBER CLEANER, MK 2.
RAMP SUSPENSION UNIT

MIRROR, DRIVING

BAG, SPARE, TRACK PINS
CLEANER, BORE, NO.4, MK.I, IN CAP SPONGE
NO.9, M.I.
HANDLE, STARTING, AUX ENGINE
LEAD, INTER VEHICLE STARTING NO.I.
MK.2.(30 FT)

TOOL, ASSEMBLING CIRCLIP
SPANNER, RATCHET ADJUSTER
TRACK PIN DRIFT W/H HANDLE
ANCHOR, EARTH, HOLDFAST SPIKE
TOOL, ASSEMBLING, TRACK
4 GREATCOATS.
COOKER, PORTABLE
4 RESPIRATORS, ANTI-GAS.
TRACK, ROPES & LINK ASSEMBLY
TRIPOD, MOUNT, M/G CAL.30 M.2. OR
" " " " " "-30 L2. AI

PLATE, SHACKLE
COVER, SPARE BARREL -30
CASE, SPARE W/T VALVES.
ANTENNAE RODS"F"CASES, CARRYING Nº2.

TAIL & CONVOY LIGHTS ASSEMBLY
2 HAVERSACKS, W.E. PATT. 1944.
(ALL RANKS)

CABLE, REEL, CONTINUOUS CONNECTION

BAR, CROW, W/H CHISEL & CLAW, 5 FT., 8 IN.

COVER, MUZZLE, M/G CAL.-30, BROWNING
GUN MACHINE, CAL.30 MODEL M 1919 A.4.
OR L.3. A.I.

BOX AMMN. -30

COVER, WATERPROOF:- ENGINE &
BIVOUAC, 5/w. 8 TENT PINS

2 EQUIPMENTS, CAMOUFLAGE NET,
EXTRA GARNISHED WOODLAND, MK.3,65
35'X 17', OR DESERT ARTY., 35'X 17'
OR CARRIED IN UNIT TRANSPORT
4 BEDDING ROLLS, EACH CONTAINING-
3 BLANKETS, BROWN, SINGLE
I GROUND SHEET, MK.8.

SPADE, MK.3.
SHOVEL, G.S.
HAMMER, SLEDGE, DOUBLE-FACED, 10 LBS.

BOX, FIRST AID, SMALL.

BOX, TELEPHONE

2 TRACK LINKS, 31 IN (SPARE)

15. 7. '57		

TANK, HEAVY GUN NO.I 120ᴹᴹ.
CONQUEROR MK.2
STOWAGE SKETCH
REAR & L/H/S

SKETCH BY	CHECKED BY	8 SHEETS	SHEET 2
G. SOUTHEY	P. Simmons		**FV.341359**
	FOR DIRECTOR, F.V.R.D.E.		

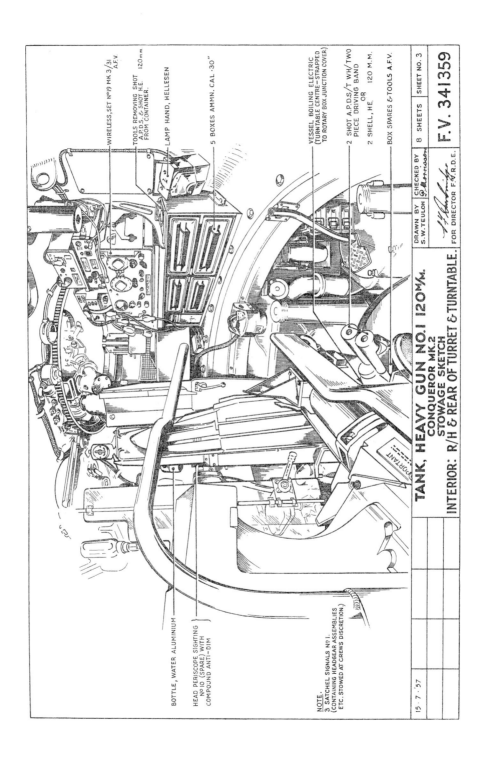

TANK, HEAVY GUN NO.1 120ᴹ/ᴍ.
CONQUEROR MK.2
STOWAGE SKETCH
INTERIOR: R/H & REAR OF TURRET & TURNTABLE.

F.V. 341359

8 SHEETS   SHEET NO. 3

DRAWN BY / S.W.TEULON   CHECKED BY   FOR DIRECTOR F.V.R.D.E.

15 · 7 · '57

WIRELESS, SET Nº19 MK 3/31 A.F.V.

TOOLS REMOVING SHOT A.P.D.S. & SHOT H.E. FROM CONTAINER.   120ᵐᵐ

LAMP HAND, HELLESEN

5 BOXES AMMN. CAL ·30"

VESSEL BOILING ELECTRIC (TURNTABLE CENTRE—STRAPPED TO ROTARY BOX JUNCTION COVER)

2 SHOT A.P.D.S./T WH/TWO PIECE DRIVING BAND
OR
2 SHELL, HE   120 M.M.

BOX SPARES & TOOLS A.F.V.

BOTTLE, WATER ALUMINIUM

HEAD PERISCOPE SIGHTING Nº10 (SPARE) WITH COMPOUND ANTI-DIM

NOTE.
3 SATCHEL SIGNALS Nº I. (CONTAINING HEADGEAR ASSEMBLIES ETC. STOWED AT CREWS DISCRETION.)

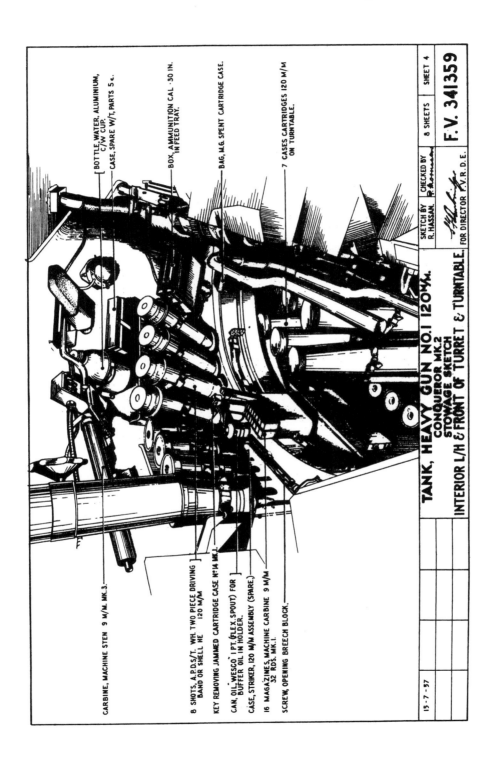

CARBINE, MACHINE STEN 9 M/M. MK.3.

BOTTLE, WATER, ALUMINIUM, C/W CUP.

CASE, SPARE W/T, PARTS 5 e.

BOX, AMMUNITION CAL ·30 IN. IN FEED TRAY.

BAG, M.G. SPENT CARTRIDGE CASE.

7 CASES CARTRIDGES 120 M/M ON TURNTABLE.

8 SHOTS, A.P.D.S/T. WH. TWO PIECE DRIVING BAND OR SHELL HE 120 M/M

KEY REMOVING JAMMED CARTRIDGE CASE N°14 MK.I.

CAN, OIL, WESCO´ 1 PT. (FLEX. SPOUT) FOR BUFFER OIL IN HOLDER.

CASE, STRIKER, 120 M/M ASSEMBLY (SPARE.)

16 MAGAZINES, MACHINE CARBINE 9 M/M 32 RDS. MK.I.

SCREW, OPENING BREECH BLOCK.

15 - 7 - 57

| | SKETCH BY R. HASSAN. | CHECKED BY R. Asman | 8 SHEETS | SHEET 4 |
| FOR DIRECTOR F.V.R.D.E. | | | | **F.V. 341359** |

TANK, HEAVY GUN NO.1 120½M.
CONQUEROR MK.2
STOWAGE SKETCH
INTERIOR L/H & FRONT OF TURRET & TURNTABLE.

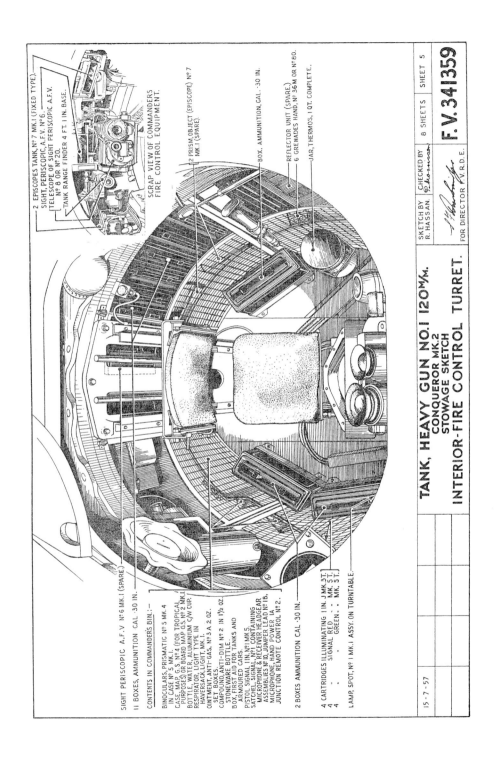

TANK, HEAVY GUN N0.1 120M/M.
CONQUEROR MK.2
STOWAGE SKETCH
INTERIOR-FIRE CONTROL TURRET.

F.V.341359

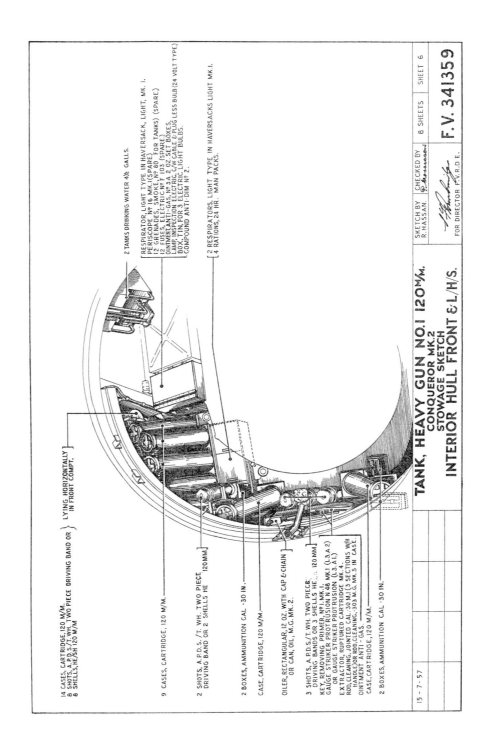

2 TANKS DRINKING WATER 4½ GALLS.

RESPIRATOR, LIGHT TYPE IN HAVERSACK, LIGHT, MK. I.
PERISCOPE Nº 16 MK.I.(SPARE.)
12 GRENADES, SMOKE, Nº 80. FOR TANKS.) (SPARE)
12 FUSES, ELECTRIC Nº F 103.(SPARE)
OINTMENT,ANTI-GAS, Nº 3.A 2 OZ. SET BOXES,
LAMP, INSPECTION ELECTRIC, C/W CABLE & PLUG LESS BULB.(24 VOLT TYPE.)
BOX, TIN, FOR 3 ELECTRIC LIGHT BULBS.
COMPOUND ANTI-DIM Nº 2.

2 RESPIRATORS, LIGHT TYPE IN HAVERSACKS LIGHT MK.I.
4 RATIONS, 24 HR. MAN PACKS.

14 CASES, CARTRIDGE, 120 M/M.
8 SHOTS, A.P.D.S./T.WH. TWO PIECE DRIVING BAND OR } LYING HORIZONTALLY
8 SHELLS,HE/SH 120 M/M } IN FRONT COMPT.

9 CASES, CARTRIDGE, 120 M/M.

2 SHOTS, A.P.D.S. /T. WH. TWO PIECE
DRIVING BAND OR 2 SHELLS HE   120MM

2 BOXES, AMMUNITION CAL. ·30 IN.

CASE, CARTRIDGE, 120 M/M.

OILER, RECTANGULAR, 12 OZ. WITH CAP & CHAIN
OR CAN, OIL, M.G. MK. 2.

3 SHOTS, A.P.D.S./T. WH. TWO PIECE
DRIVING BANDS OR 3 SHELLS HE … CA 120 MM
KEY, REMOVING PRIMER, Nº I. MK.I.
GAUGE STRIKER PROTRUSION N 48 MK.I (L3.A 2)
OR GAUGE STRIKER PROTRUSION (L3.A I.)
EXTRACTOR, RUPTURED CARTRIDGE MK. 4.
ROD, CLEANING, JOINTED CAL. ·30 M.I.(3 SECTIONS W/H
HANDLE)OR ROD,CLEANING,·303 M.G. MK.5 IN CASE.
OINTMENT ANTI - GAS.
CASE, CARTRIDGE, 120 M/M.

2 BOXES, AMMUNITION CAL. ·30 IN.

TANK, HEAVY GUN NO.1 120ᴹ/ᴍ.
CONQUEROR MK.2
STOWAGE SKETCH
INTERIOR HULL FRONT & L/H/S.

15 - 7 - 57	SKETCH BY R. HASSAN.	CHECKED BY *P. Morrison*	8 SHEETS	SHEET 6
		J. Hawkins FOR DIRECTOR F.V.R.D.E.		F.V. 341359

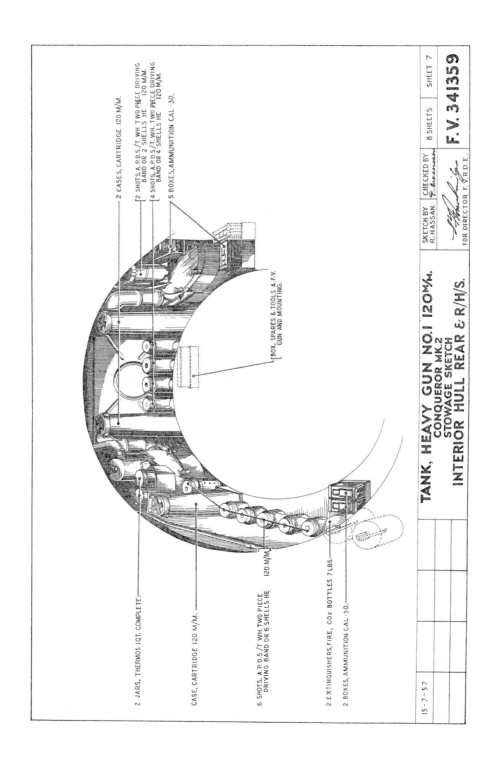

TANK, HEAVY GUN NO.1 120M/M.
CONQUEROR MK.2
STOWAGE SKETCH
INTERIOR HULL REAR & R/H/S.

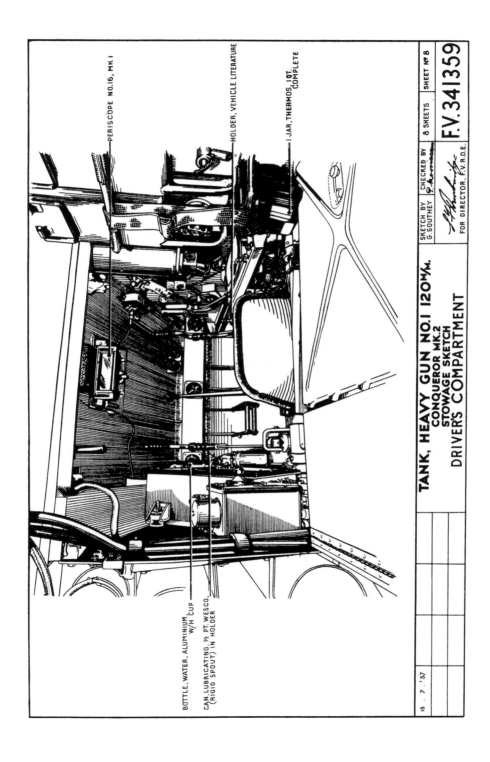

PERISCOPE NO.16, MK I

HOLDER, VEHICLE LITERATURE

I JAR, THERMOS, I QT.
COMPLETE

BOTTLE, WATER, ALUMINIUM,
W/H CUP

CAN, LUBRICATING, ½ PT. WESCO,
(RIGID SPOUT) IN HOLDER

TANK, HEAVY GUN NO.1 120 M/M.
CONQUEROR MK.2
STOWAGE SKETCH
DRIVER'S COMPARTMENT

SKETCH BY	CHECKED BY	8 SHEETS	SHEET N° 8
G. SOUTHEY			

FOR DIRECTOR, F.V.R.D.E.

F.V.341359

15 . 7 . 57

Glossary

Aardvark	Modern mine-clearing vehicle extensively used in the Balkans
APDS	Armour Piercing Discarding Sabot, a round that defeats armour by kinetic energy
ARV	Armoured Recovery Vehicle
AVRE	Armoured Vehicle Royal Engineers
B47	Type of radio
BAOR	British Army of the Rhine
BATUS	British Army Training Unit Suffield, a large training area in Alberta, Canada, used for live fire and movement exercises
BESA	Birmingham Enfield Small Arms, a manufacturer of small arms
C12	Type of radio
C42	Type of radio
DD	Duplex Drive, a system that allows tanks to float, much used in the 1944 Normandy landings
DRAC	Director Royal Armoured Corps
FCT	Fire Control Turret
FV	Fighting Vehicle
FVPE	Fighting Vehicle Proof Establishment
GPMG	General Purpose Machine Gun
HESH	High Explosive Squash Head, a round that defeats armour by chemical energy

HQ RAC	Headquarters Royal Armoured Corps
JLR	Junior Leaders Regiment, a young soldiers training regiment
LCT	Landing Craft Tank
MBT	Main Battle Tank
MELF	Middle East Land Forces
MTDE	Military Trials and Development Establishment
MVEE	Military Vehicles Engineering Establishment
PBI	'Poor Bloody Infantry', so called because they are usually in the thick of it, armed only with a rifle
QRIH	Queens Royal Irish Hussars
RAC	Royal Armoured Corps
RDG	Royal Dragoon Guards
REME	Royal Electrical and Mechanical Engineers
ROF	Royal Ordnance Factory
RTR	Royal Tank Regiment
Shir	Iranian name for their version of the Chieftain tank
SLR	Single Lens Reflex, a type of camera
SNCO	Senior Non-Commissioned Officer, any rank from corporal to warrant officer
WS 19/88	Type of radio

Index